実況中継 CD-ROMブックス

山口俊治のトークで攻略

英文法

フル解説エクササイズ

GOGAKU SHUNJUSHA

はじめに お読みください

音声CD-ROMの使い方

★付属のCD-ROM内の解説音声はMP3形式で保存されていますので，ご利用には**MP3データが再生できるパソコン環境が必要**です。

★この**CD-ROM**は**CD-ROMドライブにセットしただけでは自動的に起動しません。下記の手順を踏んでください。**

Windows でご利用の場合

① CD-ROM をパソコンの CD-ROM ドライブにセットします。

② コンピュータ（もしくはマイコンピュータ）を表示し，[EIBUNPO_1]（ディスク 2 は [EIBUNPO_2]）という表示の CD-ROM のアイコンを右クリックして [開く] を選択します。

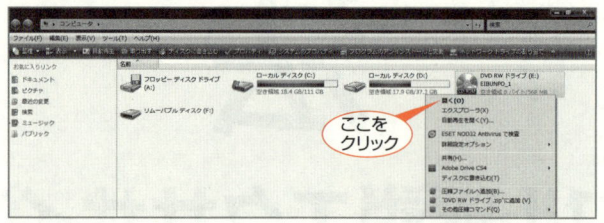

③ 第 01 回～第 10 回（ディスク 2 は第 11 回～第 20 回）の各フォルダが表示されますので，その中からお聞きになりたい回のフォルダを開いてください。

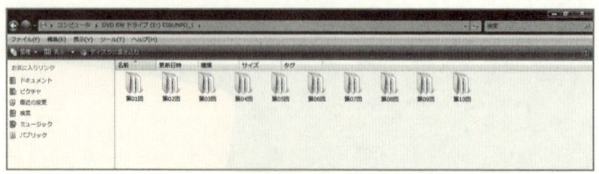

④ ③で選択された回の設問ごとの音声ファイルが表示されます。その中からお聞きになりたいファイルを開いてご利用ください。

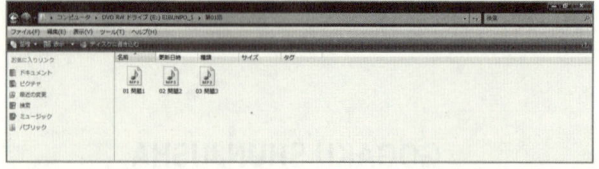

※上記のサンプル画像は一例です。お使いのパソコン環境に応じて，表示画像が多少異なることがございます。あらかじめご了承ください。

Mac でご利用の場合

① CD-ROM をパソコンの CD-ROM ドライブにセットします。
② [EIBUNPO_1]（ディスク 2 は [EIBUNPO_2]）という CD-ROM のアイコンが表示されたら，そのアイコンをダブルクリックして内容を表示します。
③ 第 01 回〜第 10 回（ディスク 2 は第 11 回〜第 20 回）の各フォルダが表示されますので，その中からお聞きになりたいフォルダを開いてください。
④ ③で選択された回の設問ごとの音声ファイルが表示されます。その中からお聞きになりたいファイルを開いてご利用ください。

> 本書添付のCD-ROMはWindows仕様のため，Macでご使用の場合，お使いのパソコン環境によって，フォルダ名・ファイル名が文字化けして表示されてしまう場合があります。ただし，"iTunes" 等で再生いただく際には，正しく表示されますのでご安心ください。

⚠ 注意事項

❶ この CD-ROM はパソコン専用です。**オーディオ用プレーヤーでは絶対に再生しないでください。**大音量によって耳に傷害を負ったり，スピーカーを破損するおそれがあります。

❷ この CD-ROM の一部または全部を，バックアップ以外の目的でいかなる方法においても無断で複製することは法律で禁じられています。

❸ この CD-ROM を使用し，どのようなトラブルが発生しても，当社は一切責任を負いません。ご利用は個人の責任において行ってください。

❹ 携帯音楽プレーヤーに音声データを転送される場合は，必ずプレーヤーの取扱説明書をお読みになった上でご使用ください。また，その際の転送ソフトの動作環境は，ソフトウェアによって異なりますので，ご不明の点については，各ソフトウェアの商品サポートにお問い合わせください。

スタートラインに立って

　こんにちは。皆さんはなぜ自分がこういう英文法を学ぶのか，これを一番初めに考えておいたほうがいいと思います。英語という言葉を勉強していくわけですが，どういう方面から英語に接近するかを考えますと，一つは皆さんの今まで習ってきたこと，あるいは今まで生きてきて身につけた内容的な常識などから見当をつけて，とにかく内容を中心に読んで読んで読みまくることが考えられます。

　しかし，それだけではやっぱり限界があるわけで，特に大学の入試問題では正確さを要求されますから，どうしても設問がついているところとかになりますと，一回立ち止まって考えないといけない，ということがしょっちゅうありますね。で，そういうときにどうするか。そうしますともう一方，重要なアプローチの仕方なんですけれども，いわゆる英語の文章の「形」ですね，英文がどういうカタチでできているか，つまり文法的なことを手がかりにしてアプローチすることがどうしても必要なわけです。ですから，ふだんどんどんすらすら抵抗を感じてないときは，こういう英文法なんてことは考えなくていいわけですが，ちょっと困ったなと思って立ち止まったときは，この文法というのが有力な手段になると思います。特に外国語ですから，漠然とした常識だけでは処置できない。やはりカタチというものについて根本的な理解をしておいて，内容と形の両面から一生懸命考える，そうしますとわかってくるということが多いわけです。

　ただ，英文法と言いましてもこれからお話ししていく文法は，いわゆる規則の羅列とか，あるいは文法用語を覚えるとか，いわゆる文法らしい文法，そういうことではないわけです。そうではなくて，つまりそういう細かい断片的な知識をたくさん積み重ねるといったような考え方ではまったくありませんで，1回目から20回目まで一貫して私の頭にあって，お話ししていこうかと思うのは，英語という文章がどういうふうにしてできているか，そういうことをわかってもらいたいと，それが根本にあります。したがって，言葉を換えて言えば，木の枝とか葉とか，そういう細かいこ

とよりも，どちらかと言いますと「幹」，大きな骨組みを全体的につかんでいただく。頭をバラバラにするんではなくて，つまり細かいことを暗記するんではなくて，むしろどっちかと言うと理解していただく。つまり英語というのはこういうふうにできているんだなということを，20回を通して系統的なまとまりを頭の中に作っていただくということが基本です。ですから皆さんもやりながら，もうちょっと大きな目で全体を眺めるというような心持ちになってもらうといいと思います。

英文法をやりますと，ただ英文法の問題が解けるといったような，そんなところじゃまったくないわけですね。これはもう英語全体にわたる基礎になる，そこをやっているんだということですから，頑張ってやっていただきたいと思います。文法によって英語っていうものがわかってくれば，英文解釈とか長文読解とか，そういう読解力の面にも間接的に，あるいは直接的に，必ず役立ちます。また，英作文をはじめとして，表現力を問う問題にも，どうしても文法的な基礎というものは欠かせないはずです。そういうわけで，全体の基礎にあたるんだと，それが文法なんだということで，基礎固めをガッチリやることの必要性をよく理解してスタートしていただくといいと思います。

最後に拙句をひとつ。
　　　　　　山吹の こぼれる土に 竹の子ら

鮮黄色の山吹の花びらが散る地面に，竹の若芽(つまり，竹の子)が勢いよく顔を出している。「土」が私なら，「竹の子」はもちろん皆さんのことですね。水と養分を吸収して，瞬く間に竹が空に向かってぐんぐん伸びていく勢いは驚異的で，強風にも折れない柔軟性もすばらしい。まさに皆さんにぴったりです。

どうか大地に根を張って，竹のように強くしなやかに成長し続けるよう願っています。私が皆さんの「土」になれれば，これぞ本望です。

山口　俊治

CONTENTS ...

※目次に掲載のTRACKは，パソコン上でCD-ROM内の各フォルダを開いたときに表示される，音声データの内容です。

第1回　動詞・文型（1） …………………………… 1
- TRACK 1　問題1
- TRACK 2　問題2
- TRACK 3　問題3

第2回　動詞・文型（2） …………………………… 11
- TRACK 1　問題1①　(1)～(5)
- TRACK 2　問題1②　(6)～(10)
- TRACK 3　問題2
- TRACK 4　問題3

第3回　時　制 …………………………………… 23
- TRACK 1　問題1
- TRACK 2　問題2
- TRACK 3　問題3
- TRACK 4　問題4

第4回　受動態 …………………………………… 35
- TRACK 1　問題1①　(1)～(4)
- TRACK 2　問題1②　(5)～(8)
- TRACK 3　問題2
- TRACK 4　問題3

第5回　助動詞 …………………………………… 47
- TRACK 1　問題1①　(1)～(3)
- TRACK 2　問題1②　(4)～(10)
- TRACK 3　問題2
- TRACK 4　問題3

第6回　仮定法 …………………………………… 63
- TRACK 1　問題1
- TRACK 2　問題2

| TRACK 3 | 問題3 |
| TRACK 4 | 問題4 |

第7回　話法・数の一致 …… 73
TRACK 1	問題1 ①　(1)〜(5)
TRACK 2	問題1 ②　(6)〜(10)
TRACK 3	問題2
TRACK 4	問題3

第8回　不定詞 …… 87
TRACK 1	問題1
TRACK 2	問題2
TRACK 3	問題3
TRACK 4	問題4

第9回　分詞・動名詞 …… 101
TRACK 1	問題1 ①　(1)〜(5)
TRACK 2	問題1 ②　(6)〜(10)
TRACK 3	問題2
TRACK 4	問題3

第10回　名詞・代名詞・冠詞 …… 115
TRACK 1	問題1 ①　(1)〜(5)
TRACK 2	問題1 ②　(6)〜(10)
TRACK 3	問題2
TRACK 4	問題3
TRACK 5	問題4
TRACK 6	問題5

第11回　形容詞・副詞・疑問詞 …… 133
TRACK 1	問題1 ①　(1)〜(6)
TRACK 2	問題1 ②　(7)〜(10)
TRACK 3	問題2
TRACK 4	問題3
TRACK 5	問題4

|TRACK 6| 問題5

第12回　関係詞 ……………………………… 149
|TRACK 1| 問題1① 　(1)〜(6)
|TRACK 2| 問題1② 　(7)〜(12)
|TRACK 3| 問題2
|TRACK 4| 問題3① 　(1)
|TRACK 5| 問題3② 　(2)

第13回　比　較 ……………………………… 163
|TRACK 1| 問題1
|TRACK 2| 問題2
|TRACK 3| 問題3① 　(1)(2)
|TRACK 4| 問題3② 　(3)〜(5)
|TRACK 5| 問題4① 　(1)〜(3)
|TRACK 6| 問題4② 　(4)(5)

第14回　否定・比較 ………………………… 179
|TRACK 1| 問題1
|TRACK 2| 問題2
|TRACK 3| 問題3
|TRACK 4| 問題4

第15回　否　定 ……………………………… 191
|TRACK 1| 問題1① 　(1)〜(6)
|TRACK 2| 問題1② 　(7)〜(12)
|TRACK 3| 問題2① 　(1)〜(3)
|TRACK 4| 問題2② 　(4)〜(6)
|TRACK 5| 問題3

第16回　接続詞 ……………………………… 207
|TRACK 1| 問題1① 　(1)〜(3)
|TRACK 2| 問題1② 　(4)〜(7)
|TRACK 3| 問題1③ 　(8)〜(10)
|TRACK 4| 問題2① 　(1)〜(4)

| TRACK 5 | 問題2 ② （5）～（8）
| TRACK 6 | 問題3
| TRACK 7 | 問題4

第17回　前置詞 ……………………………… 223
| TRACK 1 | 問題1 ① （1）～（15）
| TRACK 2 | 問題1 ② （16）～（20）
| TRACK 3 | 問題2
| TRACK 4 | 問題3
| TRACK 5 | 問題4

第18回　出題形式別・実戦問題演習（1） ……… 241
| TRACK 1 | 問題1 ① （1）～（10）
| TRACK 2 | 問題1 ② （11）～（15）
| TRACK 3 | 問題2
| TRACK 4 | 問題3 ① （1）～（5）
| TRACK 5 | 問題3 ② （6）～（10）
| TRACK 6 | 問題4

第19回　出題形式別・実戦問題演習（2） ……… 259
| TRACK 1 | 問題1 ① （1）～（6）
| TRACK 2 | 問題1 ② （7）～（12）
| TRACK 3 | 問題2 ① （1）～（5）
| TRACK 4 | 問題2 ② （6）～（10）
| TRACK 5 | 問題3

第20回　出題形式別・実戦問題演習（3） ……… 277
| TRACK 1 | 問題1 ① （1）～（4）
| TRACK 2 | 問題1 ② （5）～（8）
| TRACK 3 | 問題2
| TRACK 4 | 問題3 ① （1）～（3）
| TRACK 5 | 問題3 ② （4）～（6）
| TRACK 6 | 日本語と英語の違い・5つのポイント

索引 …………………………………………… 291

本書の使い方

別冊の問題を解き終わったら，CD-ROMの解説講義をじっくり聞きましょう。

本書の解説は音声と連動していますので，講義を聞きながら赤ペンの解説を読むと効果抜群です。

なお，音声の中に出てくる「本」および「テキスト」の表現には，『山口英文法講義の実況中継』を指し示している場合があります。念のため。

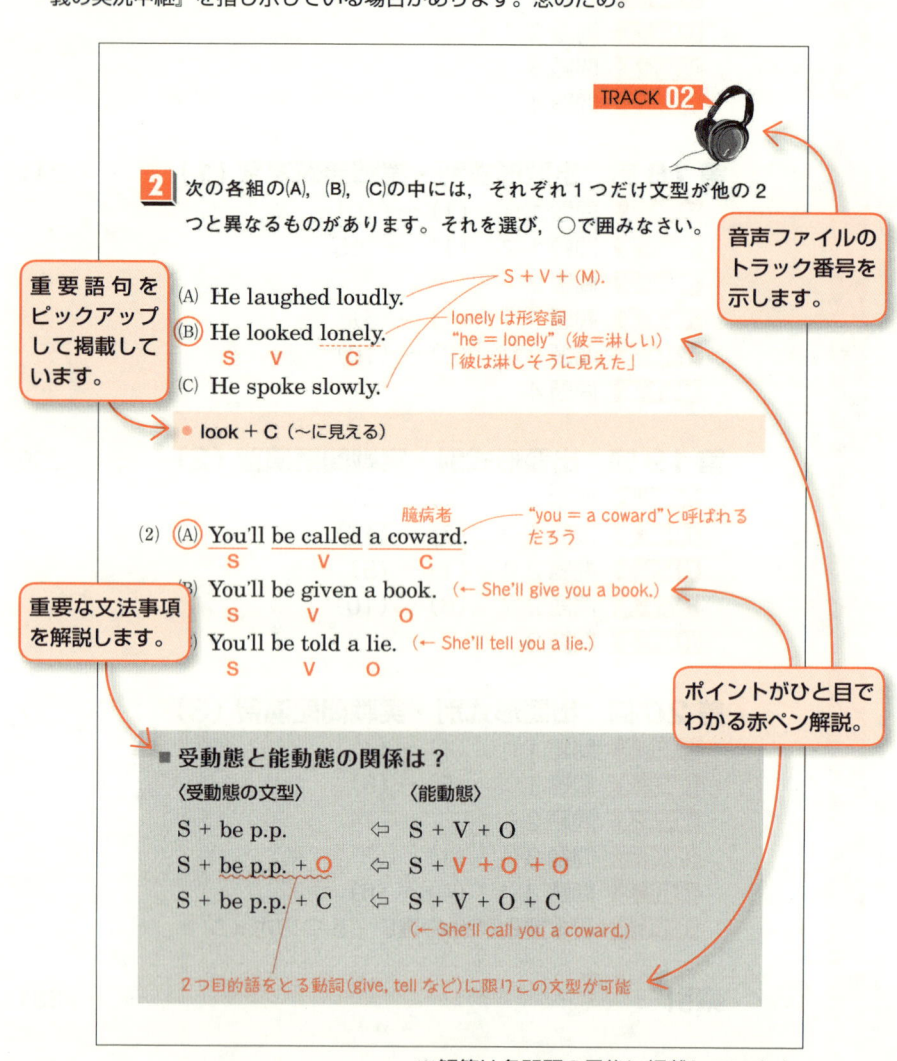

TRACK 02

2 次の各組の(A)，(B)，(C)の中には，それぞれ1つだけ文型が他の2つと異なるものがあります。それを選び，○で囲みなさい。

(A) He laughed loudly.　　S + V + (M).
(B) He looked lonely.　　lonely は形容詞
　　S　V　　C　　　　　"he = lonely"（彼＝淋しい）
(C) He spoke slowly.　　「彼は淋しそうに見えた」

● look + C（〜に見える）

(2) (A) You'll be called a coward.　臆病者　"you = a coward"と呼ばれるだろう
　　　　S　　V　　　C
　　(B) You'll be given a book.　(← She'll give you a book.)
　　　　S　　V　　　O
　　(C) You'll be told a lie.　(← She'll tell you a lie.)
　　　　S　　V　　O

■ 受動態と能動態の関係は？

〈受動態の文型〉　　　〈能動態〉
S + be p.p.　　　⇐　S + V + O
S + be p.p. + O　⇐　S + V + O + O
S + be p.p. + C　⇐　S + V + O + C
　　　　　　　　　　　(← She'll call you a coward.)

2つ目的語をとる動詞(give, tell など)に限りこの文型が可能

重要語句をピックアップして掲載しています。

音声ファイルのトラック番号を示します。

重要な文法事項を解説します。

ポイントがひと目でわかる赤ペン解説。

※解答は各問題の最後に掲載しています。

第1回

動詞・文型（1）

■ 英文の基本形式

S + V + X (+X)

日本語は「暑いですね」のように主語・動詞…を意識しないが，英語では主語(S)を使って It's very warm, isn't it? と言う。
ここを理解することが基本となる。

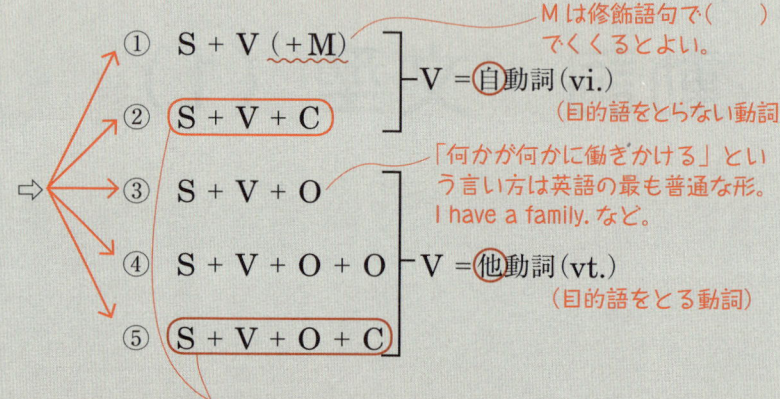

① S + V (+M) — Mは修飾語句で( )でくくるとよい。
② S + V + C
③ S + V + O
④ S + V + O + O
⑤ S + V + O + C

V = 自動詞(vi.)（目的語をとらない動詞）
V = 他動詞(vt.)（目的語をとる動詞）

「何かが何かに働きかける」という言い方は英語の最も普通な形。I have a family. など。

英語の基本的な文型のうち特に注意する文型！

■ 第2文型　問題 1 ⑷⑻⑽のXは？

S + V + X ⇨ （意味の上で S = X）ならば

S + V + C （意味の上で S = C）となる。

■ 第5文型　問題 1 ⑵⑸⑺の "O + X" の部分は？

S + V + O + X ⇨ （意味の上で O = X）ならば

S + V + O + C （意味の上で O = C）となる。
ここを確認するとよい。

(S´ + V´)
…が～する
…は～である

第1回　動詞・文型(1)

1 英文の構造を次の5つの形式に分類するとして，(1)〜(10)の英文はどの形式になるか。答えはA, B, C, D, Eの記号を用いて示しなさい。

A …… 第1形式　主語＋動詞（**S V**）⎫
B …… 第2形式　主語＋動詞＋補語（**S V C**）⎬ Vは自動詞
C …… 第3形式　主語＋動詞＋目的語（**S V O**）⎫
D …… 第4形式　主語＋動詞＋目的語＋目的語（**S V O O**）⎬ Vは他動詞
E …… 第5形式　主語＋動詞＋目的語＋補語（**S V O C**）⎭

(1) (Which part of the United States) does Professor Stout come (from)?
　V　　　　　　　　　　　　　　　　　　　　　　　　　　　S
　　　　　　　　　　　　　　 from〜はM

- **come from 〜**（〜の生まれだ／〜の出身だ）
  「どちらのお生まれ？」は Where do you come from?
  　　　　　　　　　　　　Where are you from?

(2) The governor set the prisoners free.
E　　S　　　　V　　　O　　　　C
　　知事は…　　　　　「"the prisoners ＝ free"（囚人たちが自由である）
　　　　　　　　　　　ようにした → 〜を解放した」

- **set ＋ O ＋ C**（…を〜にする）
- **set ... free**（…を解放する）

(3) She showed us a nice collection of poems.　──すてきな詩集
　　S　　V　　O　　　　O

- **show ＋ O ＋ O**（…に〜を示す）
  ほかに give, bring, buy …なども2つの目的語をとる。

3

(4) The strange smell hung heavy (in the air.)
　　　　　　S　　　　　V　　　C

"the smell = heavy"という関係だからS＋V＋C.
「変なにおいが重くたちこめていた」

(5) The amount of homework drives all the students crazy.
　　　宿題の分量　　S　　　　V　　　　O　　　　　C

"学生たち＝ crazy"の状態にさせる。
→「あまり宿題が多くて学生たちはみんな頭がおかしくなってしまう」

(6) He never succeeded (in forgetting the tragic accident.)
　　S　　　　V　　　　　　　　悲惨な出来事を忘れるのに

- succeed in ~ing（~するのに成功する，うまく~する）
  fail in ~ing（~するのに失敗する）

(7) Don't you think it stupid of her to do such a thing?
　　　　　　V　　O　C

"it = stupid"（そんなことをするのは愚かだ）というS＋V＋O＋C.
Don't you think (that) it is stupid of her to ...? とも言える。

- it(O) ... to ~

(8) They felt very cold (at the seashore.)
　　　S　　V　　C

"they = very cold"（彼ら＝とても寒い）

- feel ＋ C（形容詞）（~だと感じる）／ほかに look, seem, appear など。

(9) <u>Your information</u> will (certainly) <u>guide</u> <u>us</u> (to a proper decision.)
　　　S　　　　　　　　　　　　　　V　　　O

「あなたの情報がきっと私たちを適切な決定に導いてくれるだろう」
→「あなたの情報のおかげできっと適切な決定ができるだろう」

B (10) <u>He</u> <u>stayed</u> <u>quiet</u> (all through the meeting.)
　　　　S　　V　　　C　　　　会議の間じゅうずっと
　　　　"he = quiet"（彼＝静かな）
　　　　He was quiet. ならわかりやすい。

● **stay ＋ C**(形容詞)（～のままである）／ほかに **keep, remain** など。

(1)	(2)	(3)	(4)	(5)	(6)	(7)	(8)	(9)	(10)
A	E	D	B	E	A	E	B	C	B

2 次の各組の(A), (B), (C)の中には，それぞれ1つだけ文型が他の2つと異なるものがあります。それを選び，○で囲みなさい。

(1) (A) He laughed loudly.　　　S + V + (M).
　　(B) He looked lonely.　　　lonely は形容詞
　　　　S　V　　C　　　　　　"he = lonely"（彼＝淋しい）
　　(C) He spoke slowly.　　　「彼は淋しそうに見えた」

● look + C（～に見える）

(2) (A) You'll be called a coward.　臆病者　"you = a coward"と呼ばれるだろう
　　　　S　　V　　　C
　　(B) You'll be given a book.　(← She'll give you a book.)
　　　　S　　V　　　O
　　(C) You'll be told a lie.　(← She'll tell you a lie.)
　　　　S　　V　　O

■ 受動態と能動態の関係は？

〈受動態の文型〉　　　　　〈能動態〉
S + be p.p.　　　⇐　S + V + O
S + be p.p. + O　⇐　S + V + O + O
S + be p.p. + C　⇐　S + V + O + C
　　　　　　　　　　（← She'll call you a coward.）

2つ目的語をとる動詞(give, tell など)に限りこの文型が可能

(3) (A) She worked hard.
(B) She swam fast.
(C) She smelled nice.
　　　S　　V　　C

S + V + (M).
"she = nice"（彼女＝とてもいい）香りがした

- smell + C（〜のにおいがする）
  taste + C（〜の味がする）

(4) (A) She considers him an expert.
　　　　　V　　　O　　C
"him = an expert"（彼＝専門家）と考える

(B) She gives her friends nicknames.　SVOO（give + O' + O）

(C) She calls him her boyfriend.
　　　V　 O　　　C
"him = her boyfriend"（彼＝自分の恋人）と呼ぶ

- S + V + O' + O ｝を区別する
- S + V + O + C
- consider + O + C（…を〜と考える／みなす）
- give + O' + O（…に〜を与える）
- call + O + C（…を〜と呼ぶ）

(5) (A) He'll be appointed an assistant.
　　　S　　　V　　　　　　C
"he = an assistant"（彼＝助手）に任命されるだろう

(B) He'll be sent a letter.　SVO
(C) He'll be taught English.　SVO
←能動態はSVOO

- appoint + O + C（…を〜に任命する）
- send + O' + O（…に〜を送る）
- teach + O' + O（…に〜を教える）

(6) (A) He walked rápidly. 　速く　　　S + V + (M).
　　(B) He sounded friendly.　friendly（友好的な，親しみやすい）は形容詞
　　　　S　　V　　　C　　　　"he = friendly"に思えた
　　(C) He talked stúpidly.　　He was friendly. と同一の文型！
　　　　　　　　愚かに

- sound + C（〜に聞こえる，〜に思える）
  何かをしようと誘われて「いいね，すばらしいね」は That sounds great.
  「おもしろそうだね」は That sounds interesting.

(7) (A) I found her a very nice seat.　SVOO
　　(B) I found her a very nice girl.　"her = a very nice girl"
　　　　　V　　O　　　　C　　　　　　（彼女はとてもいい娘）
　　(C) I found her very clever.　"her = a very clever"
　　　　　V　　O　　　C　　　　　（彼女がとても頭がいい）

- find + O' + O（…に〜を見つけてあげる）　　　区別する
- find + O + C（…が〜だとわかる）

(8) (A) She will be asked a question. SVO
　　(B) She will be named a director.　"she = a director"という関係
　　　　S　　　V　　　　　C
　　(C) She will be awarded a prize. SVO
　　　　　　　　賞を授けられる

- ask + O' + O（…に〜をたずねる）
- name + O + C（…を〜と名づける，…を〜に任命する）
- award + O' + O（…に〜を授ける）

〔解答〕
(1) B　(2) A　(3) C　(4) B
(5) A　(6) B　(7) A　(8) B

第1回　動詞・文型(1)

3 各文の文型を考えて，日本語に訳しなさい。

(1) I have always thought the actions of men the best interpreters of their thoughts.

- V: have always thought
- O: the actions of men（人々の行動）
- C: the best interpreters of their thoughts
- interpret（〜を解釈する，説明する）＋ -er（〜する人）

- S＋V＋O＋C　　"O＋C"の部分の意味のとり方が急所
- think ＋ O ＋ C（…を〜と考える，…は〜だと考える）

〔解答〕　人びとの行動はその人びとの考えを最もよく表すものだと私はつねづね考えてきた。

発展

❶ 英語のアクセントに注意

intérpret, intérpreter　　思い切り強く発音する

- 日本語…高低アクセント　「はし(橋)」「はし(箸)」
- 英語……強弱アクセント　a brídge, chópsticks

❷ 日本語と英語の違い

- 日本語…動詞的な表現を好む。
- 英語……名詞を中心に組み立てる。

the best interpreters of their thoughts（彼らの思想の最良の解釈者）(!)という発想。

「人々の行動は考えを最もよく表す，説明する」
→「行動を見れば考えがよくわかる」の意。

(2) She flung the door wide open for him, / silently watched him go out, / and [not until she heard the front door close behind him] did she make a move (at all). But then she threw herself down (upon the sofa) / and burst into tears.

- fling ＋ O ＋ C（勢いよく…を〜の状態にする）
  "the door ＝ wide open"（ドアが広く開いている状態にする）
  →ドアを勢いよく広く開けてやる
- watch ＋ O ＋原形不定詞（…が〜するのを見守る）
- hear ＋ O ＋　〃　　（…が〜する音を聞く）　の形に注意！
- not until ... V ＋ S（…してはじめて…は〜する）は she did not make a move at all [until she heard the front door close behind him]（玄関のドアが彼の背後で閉まる音を聞くまで身動きひとつしなかった）という文の倒置。
- burst into tears（急にわっと泣き出す）
- burst into laughter（どっと笑い出す）など

〔解答〕彼女は彼のためにドアを広く開け放ち，彼が出て行くのを黙って見守り，玄関のドアが彼が出たあとで閉まる音を聞くまでは身じろぎひとつしなかった。だが，それから身をソファの上に投げ出して，急にわっと泣き始めた。

# 第 2 回

動詞・文型（2）

■ 文法と語法
個々の動詞の使い方（usage）にも習熟しておこう。

■ 動詞の用法
　　　　　　　　　← ここに注目。文型と関連する
S +Ⓥ+ X + (+ X)

① 自動詞（v.i.）──他動詞（v.t.）
　　　　　　　　　　　└─ marry, discuss,
　　　　　　　　　　　　　 mention など

② 動詞の活用

③ 重要動詞の用法
　　　　　└─ rob, remind, etc.

---

1 （　）内の語句のうち適当なものを選び，その語句を○で囲みなさい。

　　　　　　　　　　過去形
(1) He (hang /⦅hung⦆/ hanged) his coat (in the closet).
　　　S　　　　　V　　　　　　　　　O　　　押入れ
　現在形は He hangs his coat ... となる

- hang − hung − hung（ぶらさがる，ぶらさげる）
- hang − hanged − hanged（絞首刑にする）

(2) Weren't you surprised to (hear /⦅hear of⦆/ have heard) his success?　　　　　　　　　　　　　　　前置詞が必要

- hear（音・声を聞く）

- **hear of / hear about**（人の話で聞く，うわさで聞く）
  Did you hear anything about him?
  （彼について何かうわさを聞きましたか）

(3) Please (reply / **reply to** / answer to) this letter soon.
   　　　　　　自動詞　　　前置詞が必要

- **reply to**（〜に答える，返事をする）
- **answer**（他動詞）は **answer this letter** のように前置詞は不要

(4) The girl did not (**look** / look at / look into) me in the face.
   　　　　　　　　　　　　　　　　　　　　　　　　　私の顔を見る

- **look at**（〜を見る）
- **look into**（〜をくわしく調べる）（= exámine, invéstigate）
- **look me in the face**（私の顔を見る）
  strike me on the head（私の頭をなぐる）
  catch me by the hand（私の手をつかむ）　という表現法
  kiss me on the lips（私の唇にキスをする）

  　　前置詞の感じもつかんでおこう

(5) Somebody (**stole** / robbed / robbed of) my bag on the train.
   　　　　　　うろ覚えはダメ！

- **steal − stole − stolen**（〜を盗む）　　　を区別する
- **rob A of B**（A から B を奪う）
  rob a person of something（人から物を奪う）
  rob him of his girlfriend（彼から恋人を奪う）

- 本文は **Somebody robbed me of my bag.**
  I was robbed of my bag (by somebody). } なら○
  I was stolen my bag (by somebody). は×
  I had my bag stolen. なら○

(6) Who is your sister going to (**marry** / marry with / get married)?
　　〔他動詞〕「～と結婚する」　〔不要〕
　　She will get married to John.(ジョンと結婚する)の形で使う

(7) We (**discussed** / discussed about / discussed on) how to solve the problem.
　　〔他動詞〕　　　　　　　　　　　　　　　問題の解き方

- discuss ～ / talk about ～（～について話し合う）

(8) Did he (mention about / **mention** / mention of) that terrible accident?
　　　　　　　　　　　〔他動詞〕　　　　　　あの恐ろしい出来事

- mention ～ / talk about ～（～について言う）

(9) The soldiers (lay / **laid** / were lain) down their arms and surrendered.

- lie − lay − lain（横たわる）・・・・・・・・・・・・・・・・・・・ 自動詞
- lay − laid − laid（〜を横たえる，〜を置く）・・・ 他動詞

を区別

(10) I wanted to buy something to (remember / **remind** / remind of) me of my trip to Alaska.

アラスカ旅行を私に思い出させてくれる物
souvenir（旅の記念品，思い出の品）

- remind A of B（A に B を思い出せる）
- A is reminded of B.（A が B を思い出す）

〔解答〕
(1) hung   (2) hear of   (3) reply to   (4) look
(5) stole   (6) marry   (7) discussed   (8) mention
(9) laid   (10) remind

2 各文中の空所(1)〜(12)に入れるのに適した動詞を[ ]の中から選んで，その正しい形を書きなさい。ただし，文頭の語も小文字で示してあります。

(例) [make, do]　　　　He (　　　) his best to help me.　(答) <u>did</u>

(a) [rise, raise]　　　The box is too heavy; I can't (<u>　raise　</u>) it.
　　　　　　　　　　　　　　　　　　　　　　　　　　　V　　　　　O

- rise − rose − risen（上がる）自動詞 ┐
- raise − raised − raised（上げる）他動詞 ┘ の区別

(b) [sit, seat]　　　　The teacher (<u>　seated　</u>) the boys (as they
　　　　　　　　　　　　　　　　　　　　　　V　　　　　　O
　　　　　　　　　　　came in).　　〜を着席させた

- sit − sat − sat（すわる）自動詞
- seat − seated − seated（すわらせる）他動詞
- 「おすわりください」は Sit down, please. または Be seated, please.

(c) [wear, put on,　　It takes him a lot of time to (<u>　put on　</u>)
　　 dress]　　　　　　 S　 V　　O　　　　O　　　　　　　　〜を着るのに
　　　　　　　　　　　his clothes.　　　　　　　　　　　　　　時間がかかる

- wear − wore − worn（〜を着ている）
- put on（〜を着る）⇔ take off（〜を脱ぐ）
- dress（〜に着せる），be dressed in 〜（〜を着ている）

第2回　動詞・文型(2)

(d) [fly, flow]　The birds have (flown) (north) (for the summer).
夏を過ごしに北へ飛んでいった

- fly － flew － flown（飛ぶ）
- flow － flowed － flowed（流れる）

(e) [flow, flee]　The wild horses have (fled) from the man.
flea は「のみ」
野生の馬が逃げた

- flee － fled － fled（逃げる）

(f) [take, bring]　John (took) his wife to the theater last night, / and afterward (brought) her to our house to supper.
連れてきた

- take － took － taken（持って行く，連れて行く）
- bring － brought － brought（持ってくる，連れてくる）

(g) [lie, lay]　(Lying) on the table was the book [that
この区別は頻出！　　　　　　　　　　　V　　S
(had lain) there the previous evening];
前夜からそこにあった
it had (lain) there for some days.
何日間かそこにあった

- lie － lay － lain // lying
- lay － laid － laid // laying

現在分詞形にも注意

(h) [give, feed]　　The cat has been (fed) on milk.
　　　　　　　　　　　　牛乳で養われていた

- give – gave – given（与える）
- feed – fed – fed（エサを与える，養う）

(i) [steal, rob]　　He had his money (stolen) in the train.
　　　　　　　　　　 V　　　O　　　　　C
誤りやすい
ので頻出！
「金が盗まれる」という関係なのでstolen
His money was stolen.（○）
His money was robbed.（×）　　しっかり
He was robbed of his money.（○）　区別する！

- Someone stole my money.
  My money was stolen (by someone).
  I had my money stolen.
- Someone robbed me of my money.
  I was robbed of my money.

「私はお金を盗まれた」の
正しい言い方を確認して
おこう

〔解答〕
(1) **raise**　　(2) **seated**　　(3) **put on**　　(4) **flown**
(5) **fled**　　(6) **took**　　(7) **brought**　　(8) **Lying**
(9) **had lain**　(10) **lain / been laid**　(11) **fed**　(12) **stolen**

第2回 動詞・文型(2)

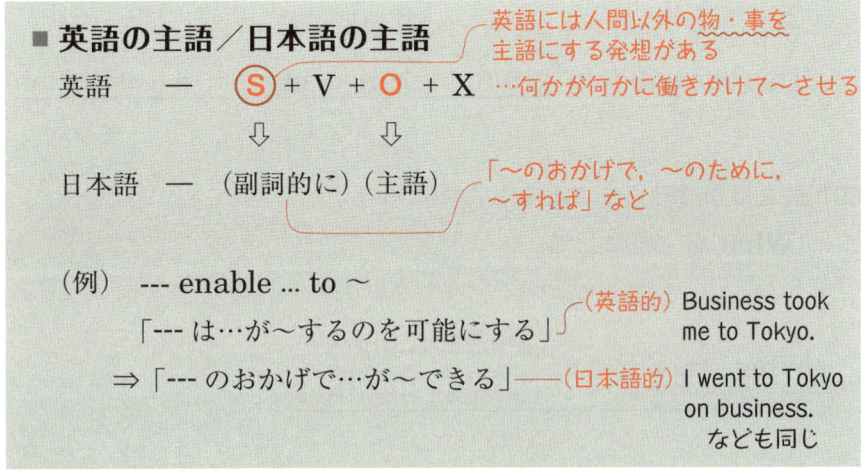

3 次の文を（　）内の指示にしたがって英語に直しなさい。

(1) 雨が降ったので私は外出できませんでした。
（keep を用いて単文で）

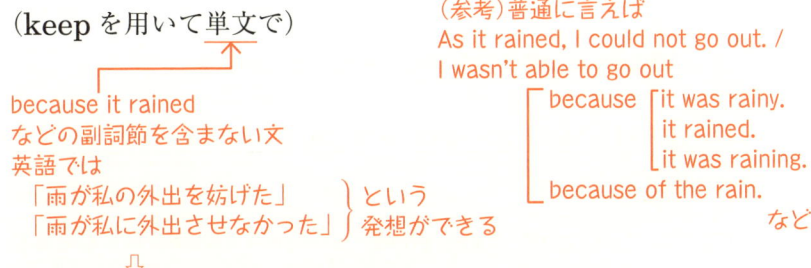

- keep ... from 〜ing（…に〜させない）
  stop ... from 〜ing（…に〜させない）
- prevent ... from 〜ing（…が〜するのを妨げる）

university（総合大学）
college（単科大学）

(2) このバスに乗れば，お探しになっている大学に行けます。
(This bus... で始めて)

（参考）If you take this bus, you'll get to the university (that) you're looking for.

「バスがあなたを〜に連れて行く」という発想

This bus will take you to the university you're looking for.

(3) 彼女はなぜそんなことをしたのだろうか。
(What を主語にして)

（参考）Why did she do such a thing?

「何が彼女にそうさせたのか」という発想

What made her do { such a thing? / a thing like that? }

どういう動詞を使うかがポイントの１つ

- **make ＋ O ＋原形不定詞（…に〜させる）**

(4) 美術館に行けば，すばらしい絵画がたくさん見られる。
(enable を用いて)

（参考）If you visit the gallery, you are able to see a lot of wonderful pictures.

「訪問が〜に…するのを可能にする」という発想

A visit to the gallery enables you to see a lot of wonderful pictures.

many / lots of

「すばらしい」は good, nice, great, splendid, magnificent…など多数

- **enable ... to 〜（…に〜するのを可能にする）**
   「テレビのおかげでサッカーの試合が見られる」なら
   Television enables you to watch a soccer game.

(5) この写真を見ると楽しかった昔のことを思い出します。
(This picture を主語にして)

This picture <u>reminds</u> me of my happy old days.
This picture <u>makes</u> me think of my good old days.
　　　　　　↳どんな動詞を使うか

- remind A of B（A に B を思い出させる）
- A is reminded of B.（A が B を思い出す）

〔解答〕
(1) The rain kept me from going out.
(2) This bus will take you to the university you're looking for.
(3) What made her do such a thing?
(4) A visit to the gallery enables you to see a lot of wonderful pictures.
(5) This picture reminds me of my happy old days.

第 3 回

時　制

TRACK 01

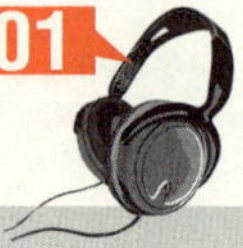

■ **動詞の時制**

S + V + X（+ X）

- ① 文型を決める
- ② 時制の変化がある ― 現在・過去・未来・完了形・進行形など

● 日本語にとらわれないこと！

「あっ，バスが来た」

Look. Here comes the bus.

「ああびっくりした」

I'm surprised. など

■ **英語の時制／日本語の時制**

- 英語の時制：客観的な目盛りにほぼ対応する（＝視点が固定されている）
- 日本語の時制：主観的，視点の移動が自由

過去
現在
未来
had p.p.
（過去完了）
have p.p.
（現在完了）
will have p.p.
（未来完了）

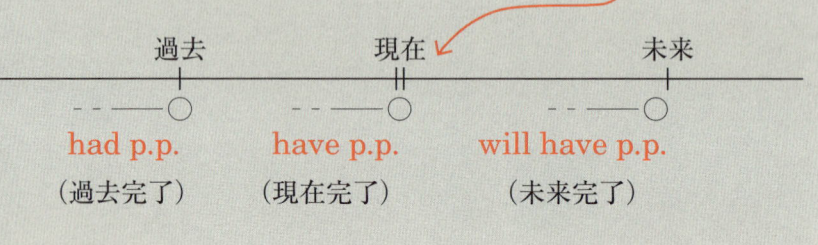

第3回 時制

1 次の英文の( )内に入れるのに最も適当なものを，それぞれ(a)〜(e)から1つずつ選び，その記号を○で囲みなさい。

(1) (By next September) Jane ( ) the piano (for three years).
　今度の9月までで
(a) will have been learning　(b) had learned　(c) will learn
(d) has been learning　(e) has already learned

- 今まで3年間なら Jane has been learning ...
- 今度の9月までで3年間だから Jane will have been learning ...

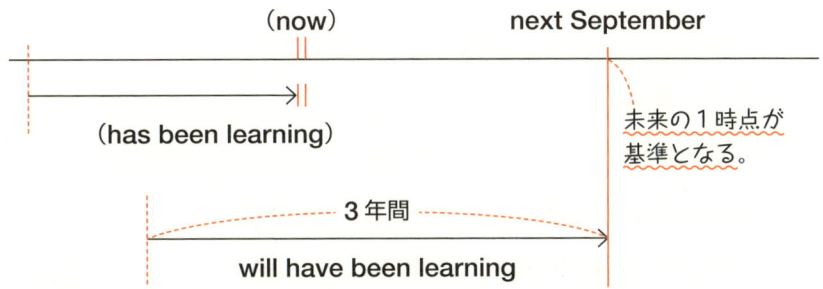

(2) Would you please give him this note (the moment he ( ))?
　　　　　　　　　　　　　　　　　　　ノート(手紙・お札など)　着いたらすぐに…
(a) arrives　×(b) arrived　×(c) will arrive
(d) is going to arrive　(e) was arriving

- 時を表す副詞節の中では未来形は使わない
- 日本語の「着いたら」と区別

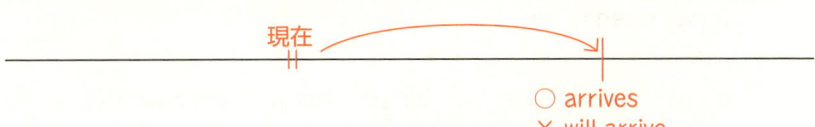

(3) The prices (　　) up (since a few weeks ago.)
　(a) went　　　(b) have gone　　　(c) is gone
　(d) had gone　(e) will have been going

「アメリカに行ったときすでに上がっていた」
なら過去が基準なので had gone up

(now)

have p.p.　→　「物価が上がった」＋「上がっている」
　　　　　　→　上がって今も高い

● since ～（～以来）は完了形とともに使われやすい

時を表す副詞節　　「仕事を終えてしまうまで待ってください」

(4) Please wait (till I (　　) this work.)
　(a) shall have done　(b) shall be done　×(c) will do
　(d) have done　(e) am going to have done

　　will have done ではない

(5) It (　　) ten years (since my grandfather died.)
　×(a) has passed　×(b) has past　(c) has been
　(d) has been passed　(e) had been

● 「…してから～になる」
　It is ～ since ...
　It has been ～ since ...　　定形を覚えておく

「やあしばらく，その後どう？」
It's been ages (since I saw you last). How have you been?

(6) We (　　　) five minutes / when we were caught in a shower.

5分も歩いていなかった　　　にわか雨にあった
ここが基準

(a) have hardly walked　　(b) had hardly walked
(c) did not walk　　　×(d) had not been walked
(e) were not walking

● **hardly ... when** 〜は「…するかしないかのうちに〜」と前から後ろへ意味をとるとよい。

```
                were caught                    (now)
────────────────────┼──────────────────────────┼────
────────────────→   ┊ 過去の1時点が基準となる。
    had p.p. （過去完了）
```

〔解答〕
(1) (a)　(2) (a)　(3) (b)　(4) (d)　(5) (c)　(6) (b)

TRACK 02

2 (a)〜(n)の文について，（　）内の動詞を正しい形に書き直しなさい。

（例1）　Mary (eat) lunch right now.　　（答）　is eating
（例2）　It is five years since he (die).　（答）　died

■ 動詞の時制による形は？
・eat, ate, will eat
・have eaten, had eaten, will have eaten　　｝6つが基本
・is eating, was eating, will be eating
・have been eating, had been eating, will have been eating　｝それぞれの進行形

　　　　　　　　　　　　　　　明日の午後に来たら
(a)　Tell it to John (when he (come) tomorrow afternoon.)
　　　　　　　　　　　　comes (will come ではなく comes)

(b)　Jack (be) ill for a few days / when he was sent to the hospital.
　　　　　　　 |　　　　　　　　　　　　　　　　 |
　　　　　had been　　　　　　　　　　　　　ここが基準

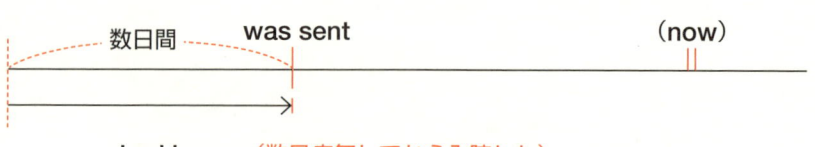

　　　　　　　数日間　　was sent　　　　　　　　　　（now）

　　　　　　had been　（数日病気してから入院した）

第3回　時制

(c) If you have heard anything from him, / please tell me what (become) of him recently?
　　has become　　彼が最近どうなったか

> ● What has become of ～?（～はどうなったか）
> 　What has he become?（どんな仕事をしているか）と区別

(d) Mr. May (live) here for twenty years (by April next.)
　　　will have been living　　　　　　　　これが基準
　　　will have lived

(e) John was ill, so he (lie) in bed (all day long).
　　　　　　　　　lay（過去形）　　　一日中

> ● lie − lay − lain

(f) Mr. White (go) to Singapore / and his place is empty.
　　has gone（行ってしまって今もいない）　空席になっている

(g) Let her have some supper (before she (go) to bed.)
　　いくらか夕食を食べさ　　　　　goes（will go ではない）
　　せてあげなさい

(h) The tears rose to her eyes, / but she (hide) them from her
　　　　　　過去形 ················· → hid（過去形）
friend.

- rise – rose – risen（のぼる，上がる）
- hide – hid – hidden（かくれる，かくす）

(i) My typewriter <u>was broken</u> last year. I (have) it (since 1975.)
　　　　　　　　　　過去形　　　　　　　　　<u>had had</u>

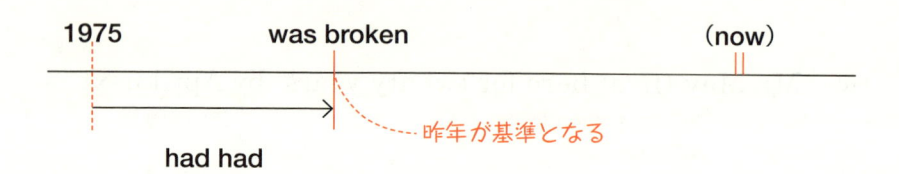

```
1975            was broken              (now)
 |------------------>|                    ‖
      had had              ┈昨年が基準となる
```

(j) 　　　　　　　　　　　　　　頂上まで曲がりくねっていた
　　The hill <u>was steep</u> / and the road (wind) up to the top.
　　　　　　　過去形　　　　　　　　　　　　<u>wound</u>（過去形）

- wind – <u>wound</u> – wound（曲がっている）　）区別。発音に注意
- wound – wounded – wounded（負傷させる）　）

(k) 　　　　　　　　　　期待していたとおり
　　Everything went on [as I (expect).]
　　すべての物事が進んだ　<u>had expected</u>（過去より前）

(l) 　　　　　　　　　　　　　　　　　雨が降らない限り
　　　　　　　　　　　　　　　　　　雨が降らなければ
　　The meeting will be held out of doors [unless it (rain).]
　　　　　　　　　戸外で開かれるだろう　　　　　　　<u>rains</u>

30

第3回　時制

(m)　My father (be) in London before, / so the experience of seeing the city was not new to him.
　　　　　　had been　　　　　　　　　　　　経験
　　　　　　　　　　　　　　　　　　　　　　　　　過去形(ここが is なら My father has been ...)

(n)　My uncle ₁(go) to Portugal five years ago. (Since then) he ₂(not speak) Portuguese, / and he says he ₃(forget) nearly all he ₄(learn) there.
　　　　　　went　　　　　　　　　　　(5年前の)その時からずっと
　　　　has not spoken　　　　　　has forgotten　　　　learned
　　　　　　　　　　　　　　　　　忘れてしまっている

```
                went                    (now)
    ─────────────┼──────────────────────┼─
5年前に行った      ├──has not spoken─────→│
                  ├──has forgotten──────→│
    learned
```

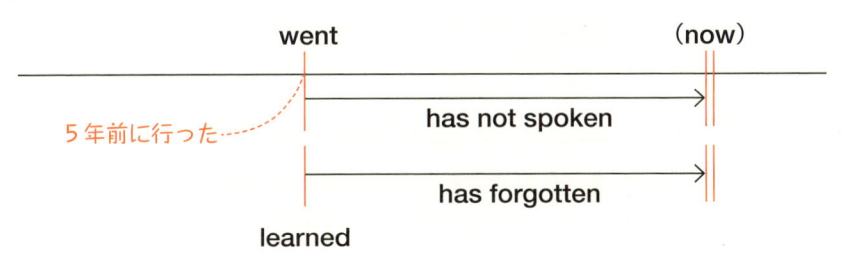

〔解答〕
(a) **comes**　(b) **had been**　(c) **has become**
(d) **will have lived / will have been living**　(e) **lay**　(f) **has gone**
(g) **goes**　(h) **hid**　(i) **had had**　(j) **wound**　(k) **had expected**
(l) **rains**　(m) **had been**　(n) 1. **went**　2. **has not spoken**
3. **has forgotten**　4. **learned**

3 (1)〜(2)の英文の意味を変えずに、それぞれ下に示された書き出しにしたがって書き直しなさい。

座席にすわるまで
(1) She did not come in [till we took our seats.]
　　　　　　　　　　　　　　　　　　　すわるまで入ってこなかった
　　　　　　　　　　　　　　　　　　　→すわってはじめて入ってきた
When she came in, we had taken our seats.
　　　　　　　　　　　　　　（入ってきたときにはすでに着席していた）

(2) They got married three years ago.

They have been married for three years.
　　　　　get married(結婚する)と be married(結婚している)を区別する
Three years have passed since they got married.

It is[has been] three years since they got married.

■ 〜してから3年になる

He died three years ago. — (has died ではない)
He has been dead for three years. 「3年間死んでいる」という表現
die(死ぬ)と be dead(死んでいる)を区別する

Three years have passed since he died.
It is
It has been } three years since he died.
混同しないように！

〔解答〕
(1) When she came in, we had taken our seats.
(2) They have been married for three years.
　　Three years have passed since they got married.
　　It is[has been] three years since they got married.

TRACK 04

4 次の文を英語に訳しなさい。

　　　　　　　　　　今より前のことは過去形

私はいなかで生まれ，／15歳のとき両親とともに東京へ移った。その後ここで暮らしており，／おそらく死ぬまでここにいるだろう。

have been living
have lived
　　　　　　　　　　　　　　　今より後のことは未来形

- come to live in Tokyo, move to Tokyo（東京へ移る）
- go on living here（ここで暮らし続ける），stay here, be here（ここにいる）
- when I was fifteen (years old), at the age of fifteen
- till I die（死ぬまで），for the rest of my life（一生の残りの間），all my life（一生）

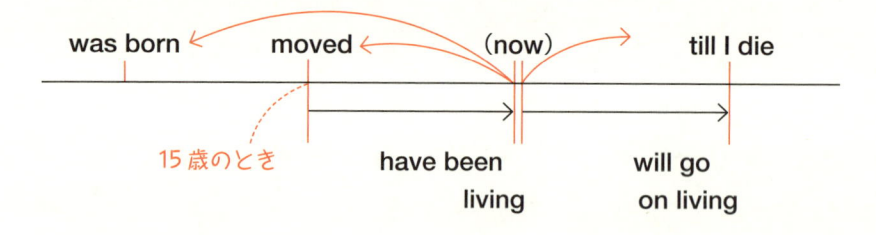

```
was born ←    moved      ← (now) →      till I die
    |           |            ‖               |
    ----------→ ==========→ ‖ ===========→
          15歳のとき     have been        will go
                          living         on living
```

- 「初めて会ったときからずっと君のことを考えているんだ」
  I've been thinking of you since I first met you.

〔解答〕 I was born in the country, and came to live in Tokyo with my parents when I was fifteen (years old). Since then I have been living here, and probably I will go on living here till I die.

第4回

受動態

TRACK 01

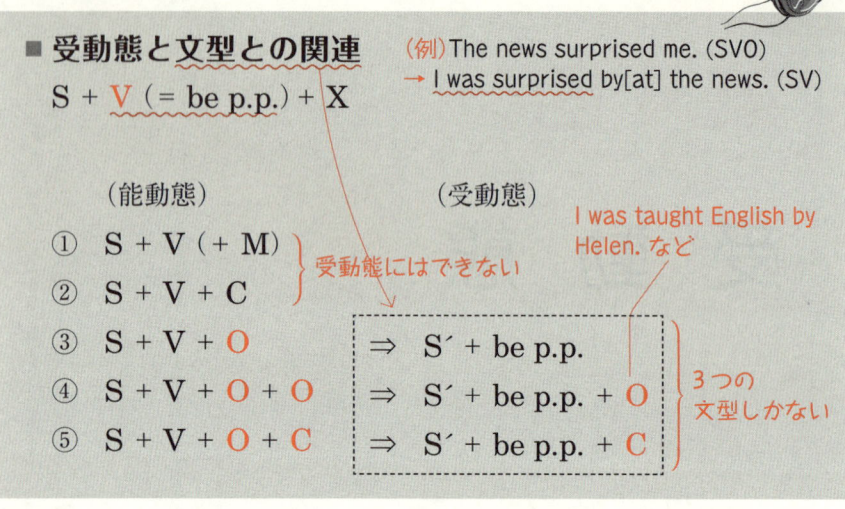

■ **受動態と文型との関連**
S + V (= be p.p.) + X

(例) The news surprised me. (SVO)
→ I was surprised by[at] the news. (SV)

（能動態）　　　　　　　（受動態）
① S + V (+ M)　　　｝受動態にはできない
② S + V + C
③ S + V + O　　　⇒ S´ + be p.p.
④ S + V + O + O　⇒ S´ + be p.p. + O ｝3つの文型しかない
⑤ S + V + O + C　⇒ S´ + be p.p. + C

I was taught English by Helen. など

1 (1)〜(8)の英文を受動態にして，下の文を完成させなさい。

(1) Someone left all the windows open (all night). (SVOC)
　　　S　　V　　　O　　　　C
　　　　　　　　　　Oが受動態の文の主語になる

All the windows were left open all night (by someone). (SVC)
複数形　　　　　　V　　　　C

(2) They are pulling down the building (opposite our school).
　　　　　V　　　　　　　O
　　取り壊し中（進行形）　　　　　　　学校の向かい側で[の]

The building opposite our school is being pulled down.
　　　　　　　　　　　　　　　　　　進行形の受動態

第4回　受動態

■ 受動態の時制による形

"be + p.p." の be の部分で時制を表す。

└ ここが変化する

現在進行形なら　is being
現在完了形なら　has been　｝ pulled down
未来完了形なら　will have been

(3) Didn't you see anyone come out?　— No, I didn't (see anyone come out).
　　　S　　V　　O　　　C(原形不定詞)

Wasn't anyone seen (to) come out?　— No, nobody was seen to come out.
　　　　　　　　　　to不定詞

だれかが出て行くのを見ませんでしたか？
→ だれか出て行くのを見られませんでしたか？

- see ＋ O ＋原形 → be seen to 〜（〜するのが見られる）
- hear ＋ O ＋原形 → be heard to 〜（〜するのが聞こえる）
- make ＋ O ＋原形 →（be made to 〜）（〜させられる）

  I have never heard her tell a lie.
  → She has never been heard to tell a lie.

- They made me stay there.
  → I was made to stay there.

  　　be forced to　｝
  　　be ordered to　｝ などとほぼ同じ
  　　be told to　　｝

37

(4) Who will [take charge of] the class (next semester)?
　　 S　　　　　V　　　　　　O
　　　　クラスの担任になる　　　　今度の学期
　　　　　　　　　　　　　— Mr. Stone will (take charge of the class).

Who will the class be taken charge of by next semester?
　　　　　これを落とさない
　　　　　　　　　— (It'll be taken charge of) By Mr. Stone.

- **take charge of**（〜を担当する）
  → **be taken charge of**（受動態）　動詞句はひとかたまりに！

TRACK 02

(5) You will have to [put up with] some troubles.
　　　　　　　　　　　　V

Some troubles will have to be put up with.
　　　　　　　助動詞はそのまま　　これを落とさない

- **put up with**「〜をがまんする（bear, endure, tolerate）」
　　　　　　　　　　　　　　　　　　という動詞句

(6) We sometimes call the computer an electrónic brain. (SVOC)
　　　　　　　　 V　　　　O　　　　　C
　　　　　　　　　　　　　　　　　　電子頭脳
The computer is sometimes called an electrónic brain. (SVC)
　　　　　　　　　　　　　　　　　　　C

- call + O + C → be called + C

38

(7) We should make much use of this encyclopédia.　〜を大いに利用する／百科事典

(a) Much use should be made of this encyclopedia. （文語的、まれ）
(b) This encyclopedia should be made much use of. — これを落とさない
　　　　　　　　　　　　　　　　ひとかたまり

- make much use of (〜を大いに利用する)
- 動詞は1語とは限らない
    You're listening to me. → I'm being listened to.

(8) They say that Mr. Jones was a minor politícian.
　　　　　　　　　　　　　　あまり重要ではない政治家（政治屋）
　　　　　　　　　　　　　　statesman（政治家）

(a) It is said that Mr. Jones was a minor politician.
(b) Mr. Jones is said to have been a minor politician.
　　定形　　　　　　　　　　　　　　to be との違いは？

- They say (that) ... （人々は…と言っている、…だそうだ）
    → It is said that ... （…と言われている）
    → ... be said to 〜 （〜だと言われている）

〔解答〕
(1) All the windows were left open all night (by someone).
(2) The building opposite our school is being pulled down.
(3) Wasn't anyone seen to come out?
(4) Who will the class be taken charge of by next semester?
(5) Some troubles will have to be put up with.
(6) The computer is sometimes called an electronic brain.
(7) (a) Much use should be made of this encyclopedia.
    (b) This encyclopedia should be made much use of.
(8) (a) It is said that Mr. Jones was a minor politician.
    (b) Mr. Jones is said to have been a minor politician.

TRACK 03

2 (1)～(4)の各組には<u>正しくない</u>英文がそれぞれ1つずつ含まれています。その正しくない英文の記号を下の解答欄に書きなさい。

(1) (a) Mary's hat was blown off (by the strong wind). ← The strong wind blew off Mary's hat. (SVO)
× (b) Mary was blown off her hat by the strong wind. ― 英語の文型にない！
(c) Mary had her hat blown off by the strong wind.

└ blow off は2つの目的語をとる動詞ではない

■ **have ＋ O ＋ p.p.** ┌ ここに"…が～される"という意味を含む
　　　　S ＋ V ＋ O ＋ C (＝ p.p.)
　　　　　　　⇩　　⇩　　┌ "帽子が飛ばされる"という関係
(例)　Mary had her hat blown off (by the strong wind).
　　　　　　V　　O　　　C

　　　[Mary's hat was blown off (by the strong wind).]

　　　　　　　　　　　　┌ 2つの目的語をとる動詞
■ **S ＋ be p.p. ＋ O ⇄ S ＋ Ⓥ ＋ O' ＋ O**

(1)(b), (2)(a), (4)(c)が誤りである理由を理解しておくこと。

　⎡ I was pulled out my tooth. (×)
　⎣ I had my tooth pulled out. (○)

　⎡ I was taken my picture. (×)
　⎣ I had my picture taken. (○)

■ 日本語の「…を〜される」という表現に注意！

I had my house burned.（○）
I was burned my house.（×）

I was introduced a girl.（×）
I was introduced to a girl.（○）

I was struck my head.（×）
I was struck on the head.（○）

I was robbed my girlfriend.（×）
I was robbed of my girlfriend.（○）

(2) ×(a) I was pointed out my mistákes by Miss Green.
　　　　　└ point out は 2 つの目的語をとれない
  (b) My mistakes were pointed out by Miss Green.
　　　　└ Miss Green pointed out my mistakes.（SVO）
  (c) Miss Green kindly pointed out my mistakes.

● point out （〜を指摘する）

(3) (a) You should be very careful of your health.
  (b) You should take good care of your health. (SVO)
　　　　　　　　　　　　　　　→ これを受動態にすると？
  ×(c) Your health should be taken good care.
　　　　　　　　　　　　　└ of がないとダメ！

● take good care of （〜に十分注意する，〜の面倒をよくみる）

(4) (a) The pássenger's money was stolen.（乗客の金が…）
 (b) Somebody <u>robbed</u> the passenger <u>of</u> his money.
 ×(c) The passenger was stolen his money.
   　　　　　　　steal は2つの目的語を　　こんな目的語を
   　　　　　　　とる動詞ではない　　　　つけてはダメ！
 (d) The passenger <u>was robbed of</u> his money.
   　　　　　　　　　　　　　　　　　　　　　　正しい使い方
 (e) The passenger <u>had</u> <u>his money</u> <u>stolen</u>.
   　　　　　　　　　 V　　　O　　　　C　　His money was stolen.
   　　　　　　　　　　　　　　　　　　　　　という意味を含む

- (a)(d)の能動態の文は？
  - (a) **Somebody** stole the passenger's money.
  - (d) **Somebody** robbed the passenger of his money.

- (b) **rob A of B**（AからBを奪う）
- (d) **A is robbed of B.**（AがBを奪われる）

〔解答〕
(1) **b**　(2) **a**　(3) **c**　(4) **c**

第4回　受動態

TRACK 04

3 (1)～(5)の文の英訳となるように，それぞれの英文を完成させなさい。

(1) このワープロは新品で，<u>まだだれも使っていません</u>。　　＜no one has used it (yet) を受動態にすると？＞

　This word processor is new; it

　　　　has never been used (by anyone).
　　　　has not been used by anyone (yet).

　　　　You have to take your dogs out for a walk every day. を参考に
(2) 犬は毎日散歩に連れて行かないといけませんよ。

　Dogs have to[must] be taken (out) for a walk every day.

　　　　　　　　　　　　　　　　　　　from far away / even in the distance
(3) 山荘は屋根が赤く塗ってあるので，/（遠くからでも）はっきりわかります。
　　　　　　　　　　　　　　　　　　You can see it clearly.
　　　　　　　　　　　　　　　　　　You can find it easily. ）など

The roof of my cottage is painted red, / so it can
　　　　S　　　　　　　 V　　　　C

　　　　be found clearly in the distance.
　　　　be seen clearly (even) from far away.

● (1)(2)(3)を能動態で言うと？
(1) … ; no one has used it (yet).
(2) You have to take dogs out for a walk …
(3) you can find it easily / see it clearly …

43

(4) 私たちが冷たい水の中を泳いでいるのを見て，彼らは驚いていました。

see us swimming

They <u>were surprised to see us swimming in the cold water</u>.
　　　　　受動態

- be surprised to ~（~して驚く）
- see ＋ O ＋~ing（…が~しているのを見る）

■ 感情を表す動詞
- be surprísed, be astónished, be shocked（[とても]驚く）など
- be pleased, be delíghted（喜ぶ）
- be disappóinted（がっかりする）
- be sátisfied（with ~）（~に満足している）
- be ínterested（in ~）（~に興味がある）

fóreigners　　make much of の受動態または
　　　　　　　　　　　　　be found convenient [very useful] など

(5) この辞書は外国人に重宝がられて，／よく売れます。

This dictionary is <u>made much of by foreigners and</u> ｢(it) <u>sells well</u>.
　　　　　　　　　切り離さないでひとかたまりに考える！　　｣it's selling well.

　　　　　　受動態(is sold well)にしない慣用的な言い方

- make much of（~を大事にする）
  make little of（~を大事にしない）
- My lecture has been listened to.（listen to の受動態）

■ 慣用的な言い方

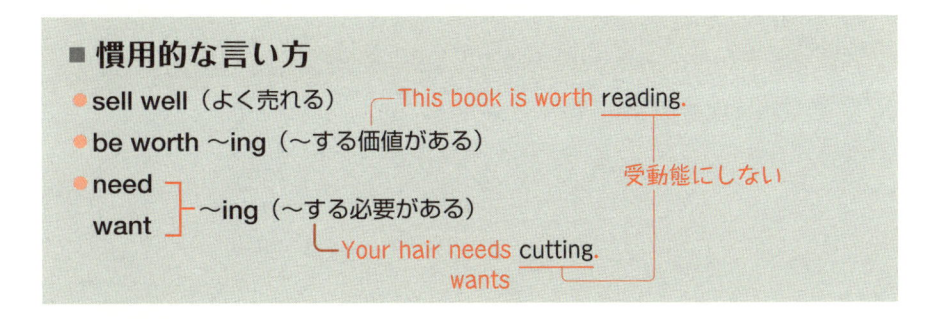

- sell well（よく売れる）
- be worth ～ing（～する価値がある）
- need ┐
  want ┘ ～ing（～する必要がある）

This book is worth reading. ── 受動態にしない
Your hair needs cutting.
　　　　　　 wants

〔解答〕
(1) This word processor is new; it <u>has not been used by anyone.</u>
(2) Dogs <u>have to be taken (out) for a walk every day.</u>
(3) The roof of my cottage is painted red, so it <u>can be seen clearly in the distance.</u>
(4) They <u>were surprised to see us swimming in the cold water.</u>
(5) This dictionary is <u>made much of by foreigners and (it) sells well.</u>

第 5 回

助 動 詞

■ 助動詞

S + V (= 助動詞 + V) + X (+ X)

① 数が多い，慣用法になじむ
② 助動詞 + have p.p. を理解する

- be, have, do, can, may, must, need, could, might, will, shall, would, should,
- ought to, used to, had better, have to, be to, be going to

1 次の各組の文がほぼ同じ意味になるように，空所に適当な語を入れなさい。

(1) (a) [Though ∧ poor,] she sent her son as much money as possible.
   　　　(she was)　　　　　　　　　　　　できるだけ多くのお金を

(b) Though poor, she sent her son as much money as (she) (could).
   　　　　　　　　　　　　　　　　　　　　　　　　ここでは過去形

- as ... as possible （可能な限り…）
- as ... as one can （できるだけ…）

　ほぼ同じ意味

may { ① 〜かもしれない(be very likely to 〜) ［可能性］
　　　② 〜してもよろしい ［許可］ }

(2) (a) John has good reason to get angry with you.
   　　　　　　　　　　　　　　　　　　〜に腹を立てる

(b) John (may) (well) get angry with you.

It is natural { for John to get angry ...
　　　　　　　 that John should get angry ... } とも言える。

第5回　助動詞

- have good reason to ～（～する理由が十分ある，～しても当然だ）
- it is natural for ... to ～（…が～するのは当然だ）
- may well ～

　　　　　naturally（当然），reasonably（理にかなって）
　　　　　justly（正当に），rightly（正しく）
　　　　　　　　　　　　　　　　　　　などが使われることもある

「～するのも当然だ」
　His parents may well be proud of him.
　（両親が彼を誇りに思うのは当然だ）
　She may well refuse to speak to you.
　（彼女があなたと話すのを拒絶するのも当然だ）
「大いに～だろう」
　It may well be true.
　（大いに本当であるかもしれない，おそらく本当だろう）
- might well ～（～するのも当然だろう，大いに～だろう）

　　　　　　　　　　　　　よく～したものだ
(3) (a) When she felt sad, she would often go to the movies.
　　(b) When she felt sad, she (used) to go to the movies.
　　　　　　　　　　　　　　（今はしないが）もとは～したものだ

- would often ～（［昔は］よく～したものだ）［過去の習慣］
- used to ～

「［今はそうでないが］以前は～だった」
　There used to be a prison.
「［以前は］～した」
　She doesn't work here. She used to (work here).
　Do you read comic books? — No, but I used to.

- **be used to ~ing**（～するのに慣れている）と区別すること
  I'm used to walking in a dark.
  I'm used to this noise.　　　｝などのように
  Are you used to this food?　　「to＋名詞」でもよい

TRACK 02

　　　　　　　　　あまりに～なので…　　　　　　　数分もしないうちに
(4) (a) The rain fell <u>so</u> heavily / <u>that</u> the river raged (within
　　　minutes.)　　　　　　　　　　　　　　荒れ狂った
　(b) <u>So</u> heavily (did) the rain (fall) / that the river
　　　raged within minutes.　　倒置形（文語体）

- **fall － fell － fallen**（[雨が]降る）
- **do ＋ S ＋ V**（原形）の語順に注意 ←
- **do** は疑問文，倒置形，強めの助動詞として使われる

　　　　　　　　　　～すべきだ(should に近い)
(5) (a) I think we ought to stop this nonsense.
　(b) We (had) (better) stop this nonsense.
　　　「こんな馬鹿な真似はやめるほうがいいだろう」
　　　You'd better ～. は命令に近い。
　　　目上の人が目下の人に対して
　　　　　You'd better eat regularly.（きちんと食事をとりなさい）
　　　　　You'd better stop cutting your class so often.
　　　　（そんなにしばしば授業をさぼるのはやめなさい）

第5回　助動詞

- I think ... ought to ～.（～するのがよいだろう）
- had better ～（～するほうがよい，～しなさい）
- might as well ～（～するのがよいだろう）
  　　　You aren't looking well.
  　　　You might as well take a day off.
  　　　（一日休みをとるのがいいでしょう）
  　　　You might as well go and see a doctor.
  　　　（医者に診てもらうのがいいですよ）
- it would be better for you to ～（～するほうがよいだろう）
- it's a good idea to ～（～するのは良い考えだ）

　　　　　　　…はありえない
(6)　(a)　It is impossible / that she was beautiful when young.
　　(b)　She (cannot) (have) (been) beautiful when young.
　　　　　　～だったはずがない　　　反対は must have p.p.
　　　　　　　　　　　　　　　　　　　（～だったにちがいない）

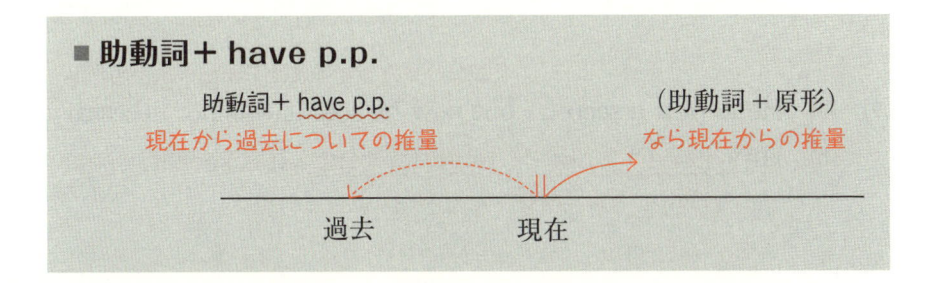

■ 助動詞 + have p.p.

　　　　　助動詞 + have p.p.　　　　　　　　（助動詞 + 原形）
　　　　現在から過去についての推量　　　　　なら現在からの推量
　　─────────────────────────────────
　　　　　　　　過去　　　　　現在

- may have p.p.（～だったかもしれない）
- must have p.p.（～だったにちがいない）
- need not have p.p.（～する必要はなかったのに）
- ought to ｜
- should 　｝have p.p.（～するべきだったのに）

51

> ● **had better have p.p.**（〜したほうがよかったのに）
> You had better have let her do so.
> （そうさせてやるほうがよかったのに）

きっと，確かに
(7) (a) Surely he told a lie.
 (b) He (must) (have) (told) a lie.
    must を思いつく

おそらく(probably, possibly)
(8) (a) Perhaps the rumor is not true.
 (b) The rumor (may) (be) false.
    may を思いつく

> ● **perhaps, probably, maybe**（多分，おそらく）⇨ **may**
> ● **surely, certainly**（きっと…だ）⇨ **must**

今になってみるとそれは不要だったとわかる
(9) (a) He kept it a secret, / but now he sees it was not necessary.
 (b) He (need) (not) (have) (kept) it a secret.
  （秘密にしておく必要はなかったのに）

(10) (a) I hurried home [not to miss her phone call.]
 (b) I hurried home [lest I (should) (miss) her phone call.]

- lest ... (should) ～
  (…が～するといけないから／…が～しないように)
- for fear ... (should / may) ～
- in case ......

  という言い方も普通

  ... in case I miss her phone call. (彼女の電話を逃すといけないから)

〔解答〕
(1) she could (2) may well (3) used (4) did, fall (5) had better
(6) cannot have been (7) must have told (8) may be
(9) need not have kept (10) should miss

■口語でよく使う助動詞
do, can, may, must, need, have to, would, should, will など

2 次の英文中の空所に適当な語を入れなさい。

(1) "Why didn't you go to the doctor?"
 "I (did), / but he didn't do anything."
    └(went to the doctor)
     行ったけど，別に何もしてくれなかったよ

- **Why don't you ...?**（どうして…しないの，…したらどう）
  Why don't you try it?（試してみたら[いいじゃないの]）
  Why don't you order it?（注文したらどう？）

(2) "Do I have to tell her everything?"
 "Yes, you (do)."
        └(have to tell her everything)
  └反対なら No, you don't have to.（いやその必要はない）

- **have to ～**（～しなければならない）〈must〉
- **don't have to ～**（～するにはおよばない）〈need not〉

第5回　助動詞

(3) "Must I eat this?" 「食べなくてはいけない？」「いや，食べなくていいわよ」
"No, you (need) not. Eat something else (if you wish)."
　　　　　～する必要はない　　　　　　　　よければほかのものを食べなさい
　　　　　（must not ではないことに注意）

- must not ～, may not ～（～してはいけない）
- need not ～（don't have to ～）（～する必要はない）

(4) "Can it be true?"（はたして本当だろうか）　「まさか」は
　　　　　　　　　　　　　　　　　　　　　　　That's impossible.
　　　　　　　　　　　　　　　　　　　　　　　It can't be (possible).
"No, I don't think so. He (cannot) (have) said so."
　　　　　　　　　　　　　　そんなこと言ったはずがない

- cannot have p.p.（～したはずがない）

(5) ～してもいい？
"May I eat this lunch, Mr. Stone?"
"No, you (may[must]) not. You (mustn't) eat lunch in class!"
　　　　（食べてはいけない）　　　　　～してはいけない〈強い禁止〉

(6) Mr. May has to work (day and night) [so that he (can[may])
　　　　　　　　　　　　　昼も夜も一日中
earn his living.]

- so that ... can ～（…が～するように）　｜ so または that が
- so that ... may ～（…が～するように）　｜ 省かれることがある

(7) His appéarance has changed so much / that you (may[might])
well not recógnize him. 気がつかないことも大いにありうるだろう／
　　　　　　　　　　　気づかないのも無理はない

- may well ～
- might well ～   } (～も大いにあるだろう，～するのも当然だ)

(8) He knocked at the door <u>again and again</u>, / but she
　　　　　　　　　　　　　　　　何度も何度も
<u>(would[did]) not</u> let him in.
　　　どうしても中へ入れようとしなかった

- will not ～, won't ～（どうしても～しない）
    This paper won't come off.
    (この紙，どうしてもはがせない)
- would not ～（どうしても～しようとしなかった）

　　　　　いくら(何度も)訂正しても
(9) [No matter how often I (might) correct him], he always made
the same mistake.　　　　　　　　　　　　　　同じ間違いをした

- however … (may) ～（どんなに～しても）
- no matter how … (may) ～（どんなに～しても）
    └ whatever … なら「何が[何を]…しても」
    Whatever　　　　　　　　
    No matter what } you (may) say, …
    (あなたが何を言っても)

　　　　　　　　　　　　　灯りがついていた
(10) When I returned home, / the lights were <u>on</u>. I thought that
someone (must) (have) returned to the house (before me).
　　　　誰かがすでに帰っていたにちがいないと思った

第5回　助動詞

● must have p.p.（～したにちがいない）

〔解答〕
(1) did　　(2) do　　(3) need　　(4) cannot have
(5) may[must], mustn't　(6) can[may]　(7) may[might]
(8) would　(9) might　(10) must have

TRACK 04

3 次の会話のうち，日本語の部分を英語に訳しなさい。

A: What does <u>the weather forecast in the paper</u> say? （新聞の天気予報）

B: (1)今夜から雨になるそうよ。

from は不要 [The sun rises in the east. (東から) / School starts <u>at</u> nine. (9時から)] — from ではない

It says ...（天気予報が…と言っている）it's going to start raining from this evening. （begin も OK） ×不要

- **be going to ～**（～するだろう，～しようとしている）

A: Oh, really? Do you think <u>we'd better</u> <u>give up</u> the picnic we planned for tomorrow? （止める，中止する（cancel））

B: (2)だめ！ そうしないほうがいいわ。

No, / Oh, no,] I don't think we <u>had better</u>.
（文の前の方で打ち消すほうが自然）

- **had better ～**（～するほうがいい）/ **had better not ～**（～しないほうがいい）
- **ought to ～**（～すべきだ）/ **ought not to ～**（～するべきではない）

[I think we'd better not ～ （△） / I don't think we'd better ～ （○）]
否定語はなるべく文のはじめに置く

(3)中止じゃなくて延期したらどう？
　　instead of ～ing　　How about ～ing?

How about putting it off instead of $\begin{bmatrix} \text{giving it up?} \\ \text{canceling it?} \end{bmatrix}$

- **How about ～ing?**（～するのはどう？）
- **give it up**（それを中止する，あきらめる）(**cancel it**)
- **put it off**（それを延期する）(**postpone it**)
- **instead of ～ing**（～する代わりに，～をせずに）

A : But when can you go?
B : (4)来週は忙しいけど，その次の週ならひまよ。あなたは？
　　　　　　　　　　the week after next　　　How about you?

I'll be busy next week, but I'll be free the week after next. How about you?

A : (5)ぼくにも都合がいいな。

That'll suit me fine (, too).
That'll be all right with me (, too).
That would be convenient for me (, too). など

- suit ～（～に合う）

    That'll suit me fine.

    (私としては都合がいいですよ)
- be convénient for ～（～にとって都合がいい）

    be all right with ～（～にとって都合がいい）

    It'll be all right with me.

    (私にはいいですよ)

〔解答〕
(1) It says it's going to start raining this evening.
(2) No, I don't think we'd better. / No, I don't think so. We'd better not give it up.
(3) How about putting it off instead of canceling it?
(4) I'll be busy next week, but I'll be free the week after next. How about you?
(5) That'll suit me fine (, too). / That would be convenient for me, too.

■ 会話でよく使われる助動詞

・Shall we ...?　（…しませんか）

　Shall we dance?

・Let's ..., shall we?　（…しましょうよ）

・Can you ...?　（…してくれますか）

　Can you help me?

・Could you ...?　（…してくださいますか）

　Could you help me?

・Would you ...?　（…しませんか）

　Would you like some more?

　（もうちょっといかがですか）

- **May I ...?** （…してもいいですか）

  May I ask you a favor?

  （お願いしてもいいですか）

第 6 回

仮 定 法

TRACK 01

■ **仮定法**

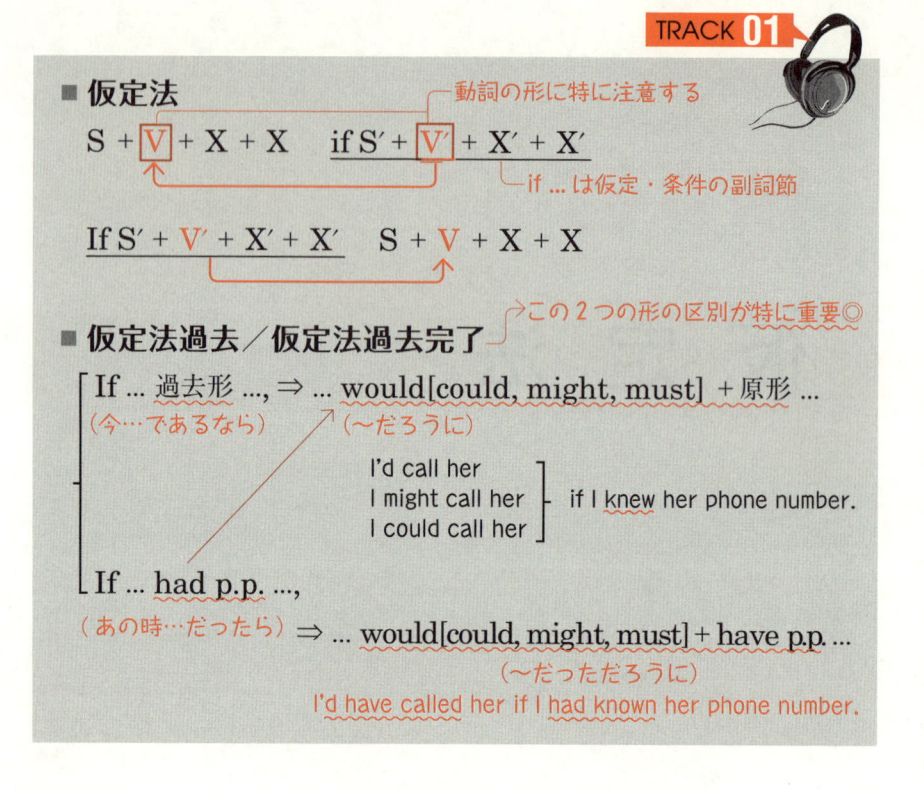

　動詞の形に特に注意する
S + V + X + X　　if S' + V' + X' + X'
　　　　　　　　　　　if ... は仮定・条件の副詞節

If S' + V' + X' + X'　　S + V + X + X

　　　　　　　　　　　この2つの形の区別が特に重要◎

■ **仮定法過去／仮定法過去完了**

［If ... 過去形 ..., ⇒ ... would[could, might, must] + 原形 ...
　（今…であるなら）　　（〜だろうに）

　　　　　I'd call her
　　　　　I might call her　　if I knew her phone number.
　　　　　I could call her

　If ... had p.p. ...,
　（あの時…だったら）⇒ ... would[could, might, must] + have p.p. ...
　　　　　　　　　　　　　（〜だっただろうに）
　　I'd have called her if I had known her phone number.

---

1 次の各文を与えられた書き出し文に書き換えなさい。

　　　　　　　　　何もしないでいる（lazy は「なまけている」）

(1) As she is idle, they will not employ her.

　If she **were** not idle, they would employ her.
　　　　　[was] 仮定法過去

　　　　　　　　　　　　　　　　　　彼についていけなかった
　　　　　　　　　　　　　　　過去　彼の言うことがわからなかった

(2) Alex spoke so quickly / that I was unable to follow him.

　If Alex had not spoken so quickly, I would have been able to follow him.
　　　　　　　　　　　仮定法過去完了

64

(3) We haven't brought a map, / so we don't know which way to go.
　　　　　現在完了←‥‥‥‥‥‥‥‥‥‥→現在　　└どっちへ行ったらよいか
　　　　　　　　　　このずれに注意

　　If we had brought a map, we would[could] know which way to go.
　　　　　　持ってきていたら　　　　　（今）わかるだろうに

■ 直説法と仮定法

I am sorry ...　　　　I wish ...　　過去形（〜であればいいのに）
It is a pity ...　　　　If only ...　　過去完了形（〜だったらよかったのに）

　　　　　　　　　　　　　現在
(4) I am sorry I cannot speak English fluently.
　　I wish I could speak English fluently.
　　　　　　　　　└（今）英語をすらすら話せたらいいのに

　　　　　　参加すべきだったのに　　　　　修学旅行（にあたるもの）
(5) You should have joined the educational trip (last month).
　　I wish you had joined the educational trip last month.
　　　　　　先月あなたも参加すればよかったのに

(6) His social position won him many influential friends.
　　　　　　　　　　　　　V　　O　　　　　O
　　　┌ 〜に…を勝ち得させた (win — won — won)
　　　　　　　　　　　　　　　　　　　多くの有力な友人たち
「社会的な地位があったために彼は〜を得られた」

If it had not been for ⎫
Without　　　　　　　 ⎬ his social position,

　he could not have won[had] many influential friends.
　　　　　　　　　　（得られなかっただろうに）

- without 〜（〜がないならば／[あの時] 〜がなかったならば）
- if it weren't for 〜（〜がないならば）　　　　　　　｜この形を正しく
  if it hadn't been for 〜（[あの時] 〜がなかったならば）｜覚えておく◎

　　　　┌ …は残念だ　　　　┌ 去年もっと働かなかった[勉強しておかなかった]
(7) It is a pity / that I did not work harder last year.
　　If only I had worked harder last year.
　　　　　　去年もっと勉強しておいたらよかったのになあ

I would have passed the exam if I had worked harder last year.
　　　　　　　　　　　　　　　　これと同じ形を使う

　　　　　　　　　　　　このずれに注意
　　　　　　　過去 ・・・・・・・・・・・・・・・・・・・・・・・・・・ 現在
(8) As the doctor operated on him right away, / he is still alive.
　　If the doctor had not operated on him right away,
　　　　　　　（もし医者がただちに手術しなかったならば）

　he would not be alive. / he would be dead now.
　　　（今，生きていないだろうに）

第6回　仮定法

〔解答〕
(1) If she were not idle, they would employ her.
(2) If Alex had not spoken so quickly, I would have been able to follow him.
(3) If we had brought a map, we would know which way to go.
(4) I wish I could speak English fluently.
(5) I wish you had joined the educational trip last month.
(6) If it had not been for his social position, he could not have won[had] many influential friends.
(7) If only I had worked harder last year.
(8) If the doctor had not operated on him right away, he would not be alive.

TRACK 02

2 次の日本文の英訳となるように，英文の空所にそれぞれ適当な1語または数語を入れなさい。

(a) 私があなたの立場にいれば，同じことをやるでしょう。

　　If I (1)were[was] in your place, / I (2)would do the same thing.

　　　「あの時あなたの立場にいたなら，同じことをやったでしょう」ならば，
　　　If I had been ..., I would have done ... となる

● I'd take it easy if I were you. （私があなたなら気楽にするだろう）
　I wouldn't take it so seriously if I were you.
　　　└そんなに真剣に考えないだろうに

(b) そんな向こう見ずなことをしようとするのは，あなたくらいのものでしょう。
　　　　　　　┌あなた以外の
　　No one but you (3)would try to do such a reckless thing.

67

> - **try to ～**（～しようとする）
>   **attempt to ～，make an attempt to ～**（～しようと試みる）

(c) もし彼が助けてくれなかったら，私はおぼれ死んでいたかもしれないでしょう。　　　┌─ If it has not been for his help, ... とも言える

　　If he (4)<u>had not helped</u> me, I (5)<u>might have (been) drowned</u> to death.

> - **be drowned to death, drown to death**（おぼれ死ぬ）
>   発音に注意

(d) クレオパトラの鼻が半インチ低かったら，世界の歴史は変わっていたでしょうに。　　　└─ low ではない

　　If Cleopatra's nose (6)<u>had been</u> half an inch shorter, the whole history of the world (7)<u>would have (been) changed</u>.

> - **short, flat, small**（[鼻が]低い）
> - **long, prominent**（[鼻が]高い）─ high, tall ではない
> - **change, be changed, be different**（変わる，変わっている）

■ 未来に対する条件・仮定

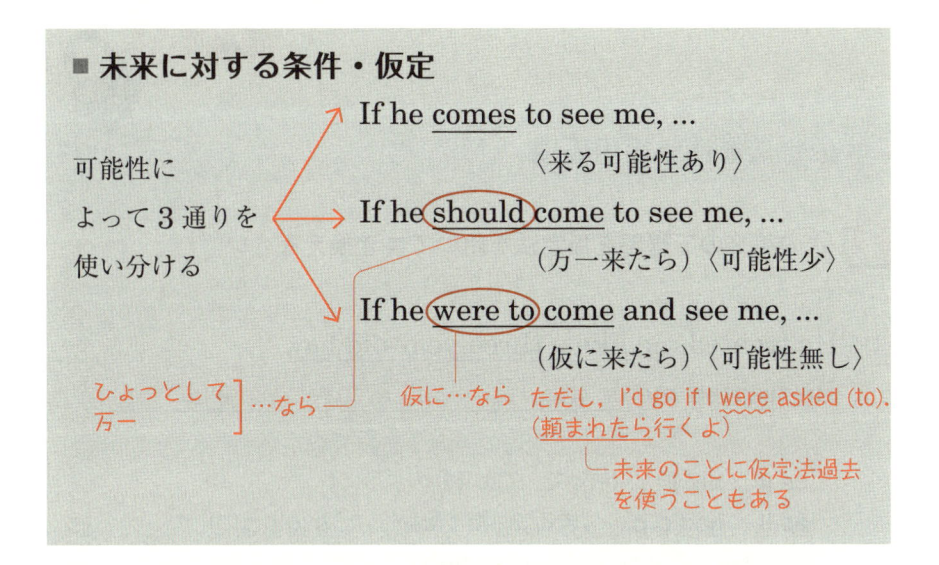

可能性によって3通りを使い分ける

- If he <u>comes</u> to see me, ... 〈来る可能性あり〉
- If he should come to see me, ... (万一来たら)〈可能性少〉
- If he were to come and see me, ... (仮に来たら)〈可能性無し〉

ひょっとして / 万一]…なら
仮に…なら
ただし, I'd go if I were asked (to). (頼まれたら行くよ)
└─ 未来のことに仮定法過去を使うこともある

(e) 万一彼が私の留守中に訪ねてきたら，帰るまで待つように言ってください。

If he (8)<u>should come to see</u> me (while I am away,) / please tell him to wait (till I come back). 留守中に

If you <u>should</u> find the coin, I would let you have it.
（ひょっとして君がコインを見つけたら，君にあげるよ）

〔解答〕
(a) If I <u>were</u> in your place, I <u>would do</u> the same thing.
(b) No one but you <u>would try</u> to do such a reckless thing.
(c) If he <u>had not helped</u> me, I <u>might have (been) drowned</u> to death.
(d) If Cleopatra's nose <u>had been</u> half an inch shorter, the whole history of the world <u>would have (been) changed</u>.
(e) If he <u>should come to see</u> me while I am away, please tell him to wait till I come back.

■ 仮定法を使う慣用表現

3 次の英文の下線部を仮定法を用いて書き換えなさい。

(1) He treated me like a three-year-old boy.
He treated me as if I were[was] a three-year-old boy.

- **as if ... 過去形 ...** （まるで…であるかのように）
- **as if ... had p.p. ...** （まるで…だった[…した]かのように）
  He talks as if he had seen an alien.
  （宇宙人を見た[ことがある]かのように…）
  （**as if ... 現在形**）... 口語では普通
  It looks as if it's going to rain.

(2) 言論の自由がなければ
[Without freedom of speech] there would be no prógress in a democrátic socíety.

民主的社会

If it were not for freedom of speech, there would be no progress in a democratic society.

- **without ～** （～がなければ／～がなかったならば）
- **if it weren't for ～** （[今] ～がないならば）
  if it hadn't been for ～ （[あの時] ～がなかったならば） ）定形に慣れておく

　　　　　　もう少し努力していたら　　　　　　　　　解決(法)
(3) With a little more effort, you could have found the solution.
　　If you had made a little more effort, you could have found the solution.

> ● make effort（努力する）

　　　母親に手紙を書いてもいい頃だ
(4) It is time for you to write to your mother.
　　It is time you wrote to your mother.
　　　　　　　　　過去形

> ● It's (high) time for ... to ~. (…が～してもいい頃だ)
>   It's (high) time ... 過去形. (…が～してもいい頃だ)
>   └ high noon(真昼), high summer(盛夏)

> 定形に慣れること。It's time I was going.（ぼちぼち出かける時間だ）
>   It's time she settled down.
>   （そろそろ[仕事などに]慣れてもいい頃だ）

〔解答〕
(1) He treated me **as if I were a three-year-old boy**.
(2) **If it were not for freedom of speech**, there would be no progress in a democratic society.
(3) **If you had made a little more effort**, you could have found the solution.
(4) It is time **you wrote to your mother**.

4 次の英文の下線部を日本語に訳しなさい。

One's memory of any period must (necessarily) weaken [as one moves away from it]. (At twenty) I could have written the history of my school days [with an accuracy (which would be quite impossible now)].

- At twenty と now の対比に気づくとよい

■ 訳出のポイント

could have written ← 仮定法過去完了
would be ← 仮定法過去

どこに仮定の気持ちが含まれるのかを考えるとよい

〔解答〕 ある時期についての人の記憶というものは，その時期から離れるにつれて必然的に薄らいでいくものである。20歳のときだったならば，私は学校時代の話を，今日ではまったく不可能であろうと思われるほど正確に書くことができたであろうに。

第 7 回

話法・数の一致

■直接話法と間接話法

話法を換えるには機械的ではなく，全体から見て意味内容を伝えるようにするとよい。

「君を愛してるよ」と言った。

I told her that I loved her.

{ 日本語：直接話法的…「ぼくはそこへ行くよ」と彼は言ってた。
  英語　：間接話法的（＋直接話法）

◎代名詞・時制の一致に注意する

He said that he would go there.

言った（過去形）　　言った時を基準にして will ではなく would

1 次の各組は(a)が直接話法，(b)が間接話法で書かれています。(a)，(b)が同じ意味になるように適当な語句を入れなさい。

◎代名詞・動詞・副詞に注目する！

(1) (a) Kate said to me, "I saw your brother last night."
　　(b) Kate told me that she had seen my brother the night before.

the night before（その前の晩に）
言った時点からみての過去（→過去完了）

● **the night before, the previous night**（その前の晩に）
"yesterday"なら the day before, the previous day,
"next year"なら the next year, the following year,
"here"なら通常 there に変わる

第7回 話法・数の一致

(2) (a) "From now on," John said, "I will do it myself."
　　　　　今からはずっと
　　(b) John said that he would do it himself from then on.
　　　　　　　　　　　　　◎機械的ではなく，全体の内容を正しく伝える！

● from then on, from that time on（その時から以後ずっと）

(3) (a) The teacher said to us, "Do you think it is right?"
　　　　　　　　　　　　　　　　　　　　　　～かどうか
　　(b) The teacher asked us [if/whether] we thought it was right.
　　　　　"…"が疑問文のときはaskを使う　　正しいと思うかどうかたずねた

(4) (a) Yesterday I said to Helen, "May I call on you tomorrow?"
　　(b) Yesterday I asked Helen if I might call on her today.
　　　　　　　　　　　　　　◎注意 { the next day （×）
　　　　　　　　　　　　　　　　　 { the following day （×）
　　　　　　　　　　　　　　　（「きのう」から見て「あした」は「今日」となる）

● ask ～ if ...（…かどうか～にたずねる）
　 ask ～ when[who, where など] ... ←疑問詞があるときはそれらを使う

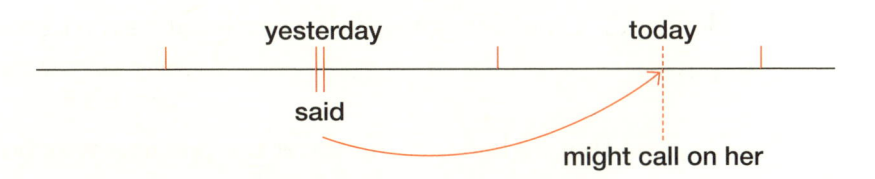

```
              yesterday              today
    ────────────┼────────────────────┼────────
                ‖                    ↑
              said                   │
                                might call on her
```

● 内容をつかむ＞機械的に変化させる

75

(5) (a) He said to me, "Don't speak (until you're spoken to)."
    　　　　　　　　　　　　　　　　　　　　話しかけられるまで

(b) He told me not to speak until I was spoken to.　(speak to の受動態)

（話しかけられるまではしゃべらないようにと私に言った）

"…"が命令文のときに使う形は

- tell ... to ～, tell ... not to ～（…に～する[しない]ようにと言う）
- ask ... to ～, ask ... not to ～（…に～する[しない]ように頼む）

否定語の位置に注意(to 不定詞の直前)

TRACK 02

(6) (a) My father said to me, "Fine! You've done well."
   　　　　　　　　　　　　　いいぞ，でかした　　よくやった

(b) My father exclaimed to me with admiration (that) I had done well.
　　　　　　　　叫んだ　　　　　　　　　賞賛の気持ちで

意味内容を伝えようとするため状況に応じて説明を加える

- with admiration
- with delight（喜んで）, with surprise（驚いて）

(7) (a) Ben said, "I met Margaret last year, but I haven't seen her since."

and や but で結ばれた文はちょっと注意！

(b) Ben said that he had met Margaret the previous year, but that he hadn't seen her since.

この that を落としやすい
これがあると正確に意味が伝わる

- said (that) ... but that ...（…だが…だと言った）
- said (that) ... and that ...（…で…だと言った）

第7回　話法・数の一致

(8) (a) My sister said to me, "Let's go home."
　　(b) My sister suggested to me that we should go home.

　　　　　　　　ほのめかす　　　　　　　　　　　　《米》では we go home
　　　　　　　　提案する(propose)　　they のこともある
　　　　　　　　　　　　　　　(「妹が John に言った」なら we でなく they)

- suggest to ... that ... should 〜　⇄ "Let's ..."（さあ，…しよう）
  propose to ... that ... should 〜

(9) (a) Bob said to Mary, "I would not accept the offer if I were in your place."
　　(b) Bob told Mary that he would not accept the offer if he were in her place.
　　　　　　　　　　　　　　　　　　　　　── 仮定法の動詞は変化しない

- 仮定法の動詞は？→ そのまま使う

　　　　　　　　　店員の方を向いてたずねた
(10) (a) The lady turned to the clerk / and said, "Is this dress blue or black? The light is very bad here."
　　(b) The lady turned to the clerk / and asked whether that dress was blue or black, / saying that the light was very bad there.　（「ここの灯りはずいぶん暗いわ」と言った）

- asked if ... and said that ...　（…とたずねて…と言った）
  　　　　　　　　　　　　　　　　　　　　　　　　[疑問文と平叙文]
- prayed that ... might 〜　（…よ，〜し給えと祈った）
  　　　　　　　　　　　　　　　　　　　　　　　　[祈願文]（まれ）

  He said, "God help me."　（神よ助け給え）
  → He prayed that God might help him.

〔解答〕
(1) Kate told me that <u>she had seen my brother the night before.</u>
(2) John said that <u>he would do it himself from then on.</u>
(3) The teacher asked us <u>if we thought it was right.</u>
(4) Yesterday I asked Helen <u>if I might call on her today.</u>
(5) He told me <u>not to speak until I was spoken to.</u>
(6) My father exclaimed to me with <u>admiration (that) I had done well.</u>
(7) Ben said that he had met Margaret <u>the previous year, but that he hadn't seen her since.</u>
(8) My sister said to me, <u>"Let's go home."</u>
(9) Bob said to Mary, <u>"I would not accept the offer if I were in your place."</u>
(10) The lady turned to the clerk and said, <u>"Is this dress blue or black? The light is very bad here."</u>

第7回 話法・数の一致

2 次の日本文を英訳しなさい。ただし，間接話法を用いること。

be back, get back, return

(1) 1時間もすれば帰るよと言って，／父は出かけて行きました。
(参考 "I'll be back in an hour or so.")

My father went out, saying that he would be back in an hour or so[about an hour later].

■ 時制に注意

I'll be back in an hour or so.
→ He said that he (would)(be) back in an hour or so.

(2) その女性はもう10歳だけ若返れたらいいのに，と言いました。
(参考 "I wish I were ten years younger.")

The woman said (that) she wished she were ten years younger.

- I wish I were ...
  I wish I could be ...
  → She wished she (were) ...
  　She wished she (could)(be) ...
  　　　そのまま変化しない

(3) 友達が，お金を取られたから少し貸してくれないかと私に頼んできました。（参考 "Could you lend me some money? I had my money stolen."）

A friend of mine asked me if I could lend him some money because he had had his money stolen./ A friend asked me to lend her some money, saying that she had been robbed of hers.

- **Can you ...?**（…してくれますか）
- **Could you ...?**（…してくださいますか） ｝何かを頼むとき
  → He asked me if I could lend him some money.
   He asked me ┌ to lend him some money.
          └ for some money.

〔解答〕
(1) **My father went out, saying (that) he would be back in an hour or so.**
(2) **The woman said (that) she wished she were ten years younger. / The lady wished she could be ten years younger.**
(3) **A friend (of mine) asked me if I could lend him some money because he had had his (money) stolen. / A friend asked me to lend her some money, saying that she had been robbed of hers.**

第7回 話法・数の一致

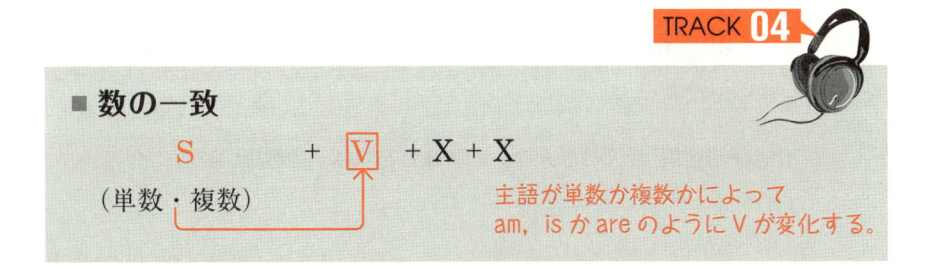

TRACK 04

■ 数の一致

S　　　　　+ V + X + X
（単数・複数）

主語が単数か複数かによって
am, is か are のように V が変化する。

3 (1)〜(18)の英文中の空所に入れるのに，最も適当な語を次の [　] 内から選んで記入しなさい。

[am, are, is, / was, were, / have, has, / do, does]

(1) Not only the boy's father but the boy himself (was) surprised when he won the race.
　　　　　　　　　　　　　　　　　単数

- not only A but B （A ばかりか B も）
- B as well as A （A ばかりか B も）
　　　　　　　　　　　　B が単数か複数か

(2) The United States of America (is) larger than Mexico, but smaller than Canada.

- the United States, the Netherlands（オランダ）, the Philippines …
  などの国名は単数扱い
- mathematics（数学）, politics（政治[学]）, physics（物理学）, economics（経済[学]）…
  などはすべて単数扱い

　　　　　　　　知能の高い人たちが試験で最良の成績をとるとは限らない
(3) The intelligent (do) not always get the best marks in exams.
　　(intelligent people)

- "the ＋形容詞"が「〜な人々」の意味であれば，複数扱い。

　　　　　　　　　　　　　　自分たちのしたことを残念とは思っていない
(4) Neither Margaret nor I (am) sorry for what we have done.

- neither A nor B（AもBも…でない）
  A or B, either A or B（AかBかいずれか一方）　｝Vに近い方
  Are you or your brother coming?

(5) There (were), [when the party was over and everyone had left for home], only two sandwiches left on the table.
　　　　　　　　　S(複数形)「2つのサンドウィッチだけしか残されていなかった」

- There V ＋ S.　← SがVより後にある場合

(6) [When I went in], the black and white kitten (was) asleep on the sofa.
　　　　　　　　　　　　　　　S(単数)　　　　　　　　V

- a black and white cat（1匹の白黒の猫）→単数
  a black cat and a white one（黒猫と白猫）→複数
- a poet and novelist（詩人で小説家の人）→単数

第7回 話法・数の一致

(7) A number of people from abroad (were) studying at this college in 1990.

- a number of 〜（[ある程度]多くの〜）→通例, 複数扱い
- the number of 〜（〜の数）→単数扱い

(8) Mr. Jones [together with his wife and children] (has) been sick (since last week).

- A [(together) with B]
  → A が単数か複数か   A lovely girl with a boy is ...

(9) It is too expensive. Fifty dollars (is) more than I can pay.
50 ドルという金額（→単数扱い）

(10) Three hundred and sixty-five days (are) equal to one year.
〜に等しい

(11) Ham and eggs (is) a common breakfast in the United States.
（1つの）ハムエッグ（ハムと卵ではない）

- A and B　→通例は複数扱い, ただし
  bread and butter, toast and butter（バターを塗ったトースト）
  →単数扱い

(12) I was told that the number of tickets (was) limited.
限られていた

83

(13) The doghouse was painted blue / and inside (were) seven puppies.
　　　　　　　　　　　　　　　　　　　　　　　　　　V
　　　　　　　　　　　　　　　　　　　　　　　　　　　　　S

- 副詞＋V＋S →主語が動詞の後のこともある

(14) Many a popular movie star (is) used to receiving many letters from his or her fans.
　　　　　　　　　　　　　　　　　　　　〜することに慣れている

- many 〜s（多くの）　→複数扱い
- many a 〜（多くの）　→単数扱い

(15) I [as well as my brother] (am) going to participate in the game tomorrow.
　　　　　　　　　　　　　　　　　　　　　　　　　　　〜に参加する

- B [as well as A]（A ばかりか B も）
- not only A but B（A ばかりか B も）
} B が単数か複数か

　　　　悪いのは私です　　　　　　　あなたは間違っていない
(16) It is I that (am) to blame ; you are not in the wrong.
　　　　　　　　　　　I am to blame.（私が責められるべきだ，悪い）

- it is ... that ...（強調構文）は it is ... that ...を取り除いた元の文を考える。

(17)　Each of us (has) a personality (different from all others).
　　　　　　　　　　　　　　　　　　　　　他の人たちとは異なる性格

- **each, every** 〜は単数扱い

(18)　Jiro is one of those students [who (have) not done the homework].

- **one of those students who** ... （who の先行詞は students）

〔解答〕
(1) **was**　　(2) **is**　　(3) **do**　　(4) **am**　　(5) **were**　　(6) **was**
(7) **were**　(8) **has**　(9) **is**　　(10) **are**　(11) **is**　　(12) **was**
(13) **were**　(14) **is**　(15) **am**　(16) **am**　(17) **has**　(18) **have**

第 8 回

不定詞

■ 不定詞の用法

（文の構成要素）

S + V + X + X　　　　　　S + V + O + X
To ...　　　　　　　　　　to ...
It .... to ...　　　　　　　it .... to ...
　　（主語になる）　　　　　　　（目的語になる）

S + V + C　　　　　　　　S + V + O + C
　　to ...　　　　　　　　　　　　to ...
　　（補語に使われる）　　　　　　原形不定詞

（形容詞的）　N + to ...　　名詞を修飾する

　　　　　　　　　　　　　形容詞を修飾する
（副詞的）　Adj. + to ...　　　S + V + X + X to ...

　　　　　　Adv. + to ...　　副詞を修飾する

（V／Adj. と結びつく）
　have to ... / be going to ... / seem to ... / be said to ... /
　happen to ...（たまたま…する）/
　be likely to ...（…になりそうだ，…らしい）

■ 慣用的な不定詞

　to tell (you) the truth（実を言うと）/
　to be frank (with you)（率直に言って）/
　to change the subject（話題を変えると）…など

第8回　不定詞

1 (1)〜(10)の各文を（　）内の指示にしたがって書き換え，下の英文を完成させなさい。

(1) It is time (I was going). （単文に）　※（本来なら）出かけてもいい時間だ
　　It is time for me to go.　※私が出かける

> ● for ... to 〜　（…が〜する）
>   　(S' + V')

(2) We can drive a small car more easily than a large one.
　　　　　　　　　　　　　　　　　　　　（A small car を主語に）
　　A small car is easier to drive than a large one.
　　※運転しやすい　　　　　　　※形容詞を修飾する副詞的用法
　　　　　　　　　　　　　　　　It is easy to read this book.
　　　　　　　　　　　　　　　　→ This book is easy to read.

(3) You are very kind to say so. （It で始まる文に）
　　It is very kind of you to say so.
　　※あなたが親切(You are kind to say so.)

> ● kind, careless（不注意な），stupid（まぬけな），foolish（愚かな）などは，いずれも人間を主語に使える形容詞
>   it is ... of you to 〜
>   　　　for you でなく of you

(4) It happened that John met Lucy in Paris. （John を主語に）
　　John happened to meet Lucy in Paris.

- **it happened that ...**（たまたま…した）
- **happen to ～**（たまたま～する）

　　　　　現在形・・・・・・・・・・・・・・・・・・・・・過去形
(5) It is said / that the report had a lot of mistakes.　（単文に）

　　The report is said to have had a lot of mistakes.
　　　　　　（多くの誤りがあったと言われている）

- **to have p.p.**（完了形の to 不定詞）
  It is said that the report has a lot of mistakes. なら
  → The report is said to have a lot of mistakes.

　　　　ドアを押して開けた　　　　彼女が入れるように
(6) He pushed the door open [so that she could enter].
　　　　　V　　　O　　　C
　　　　　　　　　　　　　　　　　　　（不定詞を用いて）

　　He pushed the door open for her to enter.
　　　　　　　　　　　　　　　彼女が入れるように

　　　　　　　　　　　　　　　　　　　　優勝する
(7) It is likely that our soccer team will win the chámpionship.
　　　　　　　　　　　　　　　（Our soccer team を主語に）

　　Our soccer team is likely to win the championship.

- **it is likely that ...**（…しそうだ，多分…だろう）
- **be likely to ～**（～しそうだ）

第8回 不定詞

(8) Life is so short / that we cannot be interested in everything.
　　　　　　　　　　　　　　　　——部分否定——
　　　　　　　　すべてに興味を持つわけにはいかない　（too を用いて）

Life is too short for us to be interested in everything.

> - so ... that ... cannot ~（あまり…なので~できない）
> - too ... to ~（~するには…すぎる，…すぎて~できない）
>   The book is ｢too hard for me to read.
>   　　　　　　 ｣so hard that I cannot read it.
>   　　　　　　　　　　　　　　　　　ここにも注意

(9) Care of the health is a matter of primary importance.
　　　　　　　　　　　　　　　　　　　　非常に重要な
　　　　　　　　　　　　　　　　　　　　[of secondary importance
　　　　　　　　　　　　　　　　　　　　なら「二次的に重要な，
　　　　　　　　　　　　　　　　　　　　あまり重要ではない」]
　　　　　　　　　　　　　　　　　　　　　　　　　　（It を主語に）

It is a matter of primary importance / to take care of the health.
　　　　　　　　　　　　　　　　　　　　　　　健康に留意する

> - it(S) ... to ~（~することは…）it は形式主語

(10) 今日では　　　　（専門的な）職業　　　　慣習, 習慣
　　 Nowadays girls learn a profession, too. This is the custom.
　　　　　　　　　　　　　　　　　　　　（2つの文を1文に）

Nowadays it is the custom / for girls to learn a profession, too.
　　　　　　　　　　　　　　S' + V'（女性が~を身につけるのは…）

> - it(S) ... for ... to ~（…が~することは…だ）

〔解答〕
(1) It is time <u>for me to go.</u>
(2) A small car is <u>easier to drive than a large one.</u>
(3) It is very kind <u>of you to say so.</u>
(4) John happened <u>to meet Lucy in Paris.</u>
(5) The report <u>is said to have had a lot of mistakes.</u>
(6) He pushed the door open <u>for her to enter.</u>
(7) Our soccer team <u>is likely to win the championship.</u>
(8) Life is <u>too short for us to be interested in everything.</u>
(9) It is a matter of primary importance <u>to take care of the health.</u>
(10) Nowadays it is the custom <u>for girls to learn a profession, too.</u>

第8回 不定詞

2 次の各文の空所に適当な1語を入れなさい。ただし，何も入れる必要がない場合には，×を記入しなさい。

(1) You may come if you want (to).　　**come は省略**

- if you want **to** / if you like **to** (よろしかったら) という形に慣れる。
- I'm glad to (come) (喜んでうかがいます)
  (例)　Would you like to come and have fun?
  　　　— Thanks, I'm glad to.
  I'll be very happy to (come). (喜んでうかがいます)
- I'd love to, but ... / I'd like to, but ... (…したいのですが[できません])
  I'd love to, but I just can't. [I have an appointment with a dentist. / I'm very tired right now.　など]

(2) I thought (it) better / not to say anything to him.
　　　V　　O　　C　　　何も言わないほうがよいと思った

(I thought that it was better not to ～. とも言える)

- **it (O) ... to ～**（～することを…）　it は形式目的語

(3) Nancy does nothing but (×) cry (all day).
　　　　一日中泣いてばかり　　　　　原形不定詞

- **do nothing but ～**（～する以外は何もしない，～してばかり）

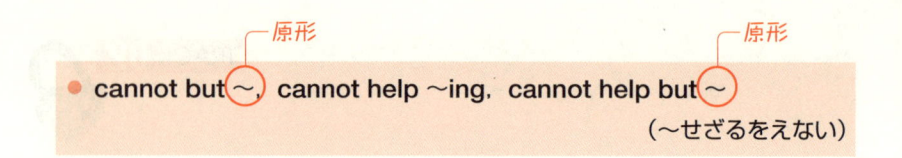

- cannot but 〜, cannot help 〜ing, cannot help but 〜
  （原形）（原形）
  (〜せざるをえない)

(4) The refugées had neither houses (to live (in)) nor food to eat.
   難民
   住む家も食べるものもなかった

- 形容詞用法の不定詞で前置詞が必要な場合
  houses to live in / a chair to sit on
  [live a house (×)
  [live in a house (○)

(5) He waited (a moment) (for) her to speak, / but she said nothing.
   彼女が話すのを待った

- wait for ... to 〜 （…が〜するのを待つ）
  wait for a bus to come
  wait for her letter to arrive　など

(6) John was very excited; I could feel his heart (×) beat.
   　　　　　　　　　　　　　　V　　　O　　　　原形
   心臓がどきどきするのを感じた

- feel ＋ O ＋原形不定詞（…が〜するのを感じる）

(7) Mary's father [was kind (enough) to take us all to the réstaurant.
   [was so kind as to 〜
   [親切にも〜してくれた

- ... enough to 〜, so ... as to 〜 （〜するくらい…）

〔解答〕
(1) **to**　(2) **it**　(3) **×**　(4) **in**　(5) **for**　(6) **×**　(7) **enough**

3 下線を引いた不定詞に注意して，全文を日本語に訳しなさい。

(1) [Thinking she would be nervous / at meeting a strange man (in
　　　　　　　～を気にするだろうと思って　　　　　見知らぬ人

such a lonely place / in the dark),] I stepped aside (a good way),
　　　　　　　　　　　　　　　　　　　S　　V　　　　　かなり
　　　　　　　　　　　　　　　　　　　　横にどいた

[so as to give her plenty of room to pass.]　　かなり
　　　　V'　　O'　　　O　　　　　　　　　　　　十分
～するように　　　　　　　　　　　　　　　　　　たっぷりと
～するために　　通るたっぷりの余地
　　　　　　　（room は部屋ではない）
　　　　　　　　　　no room to sleep in

- **so as to ～**（～するように）
- **in order to ～**（～するために）
- **a good way**（かなり[の距離]）/ **for a good while**（かなりの間）/
  a good deal of（かなりの量の）…
- **plenty of room to pass**（通るのにたっぷりな余地）/
  room for three cars（車3台分のスペース）/
  plenty of room for impróvement（改変の余地）…

〔解答〕　こんなさみしい場所で暗くなってから見知らぬ男の人と出会って彼女が
　　　　こわがるだろうと思ったので，私はかなり横へのき，彼女が通る余地をたっ
　　　　ぷり与えてあげるようにした。

(2) Night was closing in, / and (after a good meal) we got back to
   夜が迫っていた
                                        (眠るために横になる)→横になって眠った(○)
our room / and lay down to sleep. We awoke (next morning) / to
                                         目をさます(awake − awoke −
                                         awoken[awakened])
find the sky still clear and the sea smoother.
 V'   O'   C'   O'   C'
     空がまだ晴れている   海が静かになっている
     (のに気づいた)   (のに気づいた)

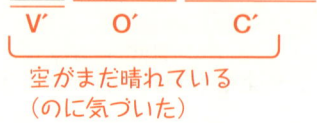

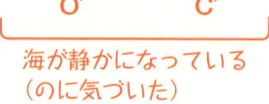

● lie down to sleep （眠ろうと横たわる→横たわって眠る）

■ **結果を表す不定詞**
● awake (to) find ... （目をさまして…に気づく）
  live (to) be a hundred years old
              （生きて 100 歳になる→100 歳まで生きる）
  grow up (to) be ... （成長して…になる）
    grow up to be a sociable man （成長して社交的な人間となる）
  （自分の意志ではなく）自然と目がさめる（生きる，成長する）という感じ
● ... only (to) ～ （…したが～するだけだった）
    try only to fail （やってみるが失敗する）
  ... never (to) ～ （…したが～できなかった）
● A and B combine (to) form C. （AとBが結合してCを形成する）
    Hydrogen and oxygen combine to form water.
    （水素と酸素が結合して水となる）

〔解答〕 夜のとばりが迫り，おいしい食事をすませてから私たちは部屋にもどって，横になって眠った。翌朝目ざめてみると，空はまだ晴れており，海はいっそうおだやかになっていた。

TRACK 04

4 各文の英訳となるように（ ）内の語句を用いて英文を完成させなさい。ただし，それぞれ不足している1語を補うこと。

(1) 何と言ったらよいのか彼はまったく困ってしまった。
 what to say　　　be quite at a loss
 (a, at, loss, quite, say, to, was)
 He was quite at a loss what to say.
 （what I should say の意）

■ 疑問詞＋to ～

- be at a loss what to say（何と言ってよいか途方にくれる）

- how to ～（どう～すべきか，～のしかた）

 whom to ～（誰を～すべきか）
  whom to choose（誰を選んだらよいか）

 when to ～（いつ～したらよいか）
  when to leave（いつ出発したらいいか）

 where to ～（どこへ／どこで～したらいいか）
  where to go（どこへ行けばいいか）

 which book to read（どっちの本を読んだらいいか）
 which way to go（どっちへ行ったらよいか）
 whether to ～ (or not)（～すべきかどうか）

97

(2) 彼が自分のあやまちを告白するのを聞いて, 私たちは大いに驚いた。
(conféss, were, hear, his, fault, astónished, to)
We were astonished to hear him confess his fault.
　　　　　　　　　　　　　V'　O'　C'（原形不定詞）

- **be astonished to ～**（～して大いに驚く）
- **be surprised to ～**（～して驚く）
- **be happy to ～**（喜んで～する）
   I'll be happy to come.
- **hear ＋ O ＋原形不定詞**（…が～するのを聞く）

　　　　　　　　この語に注目して the last ... to ～とする
(3) ロバートは決してうそを言うような男ではありません。
(a, is, last, lie, man, tell, the)
Robert is the last man to tell a lie.
　　　　is most unlikely to tell a lie.

- **the last ... to ～**（とうてい～する…ではない）強い否定
   He is the last man to be loved by girls.
   （女の子にとても愛されそうもない男だ）
- **be (most) unlikely to ～**（とても～しそうにない）

(4) 日本人が(発音も文法も日本語とまったく違う)英語をものにするのはなかなか大変だ。

(and, different, English, from, grámmar, in, is, Japanese, Japanese people, master, pronúnciation, to, which)

語尾のスペリングに注意

スペリングに注意　pronounce(発音する)

It is very hard for Japanese people to master English, which is different from Japanese in pronunciation and grammar.

- it(S) ... for ... to ～ (…が～するのは…だ)
- grámmar, séminar, cálendar, ... →語尾 -ar に注意
- pronóunce (発音する), pronúnciation (発音)→スペリングを区別
  renóunce (放棄する), renúnciation (放棄)— renunciation of war
  　　　　　　　　　　　　　　　　　　　　　　(戦争放棄)
- heterogéneous (異種の, 異質の), homogéneous (同質の, 同種の)

生まれが複雑なのは英語の特徴
　　Anglo-Saxon　＋　外来語多数　→発音・スペリングの不一致
(アングロサクソン語)　(ラテン語, ギリシャ語, ドイツ語…)

- 日本語：高低アクセント(橋と箸など)
  英　語：強弱アクセント(brídge, chópsticks など)

〔解答〕
(1) He was quite at a loss what to say.
(2) We were astonished to hear him confess his fault.
(3) Robert is the last man to tell a lie.
(4) It is very hard for Japanese people to master English, which is different from Japanese in pronunciation and grammar.

第9回

分詞・動名詞

不定詞・分詞・動名詞は文の構成要素となる

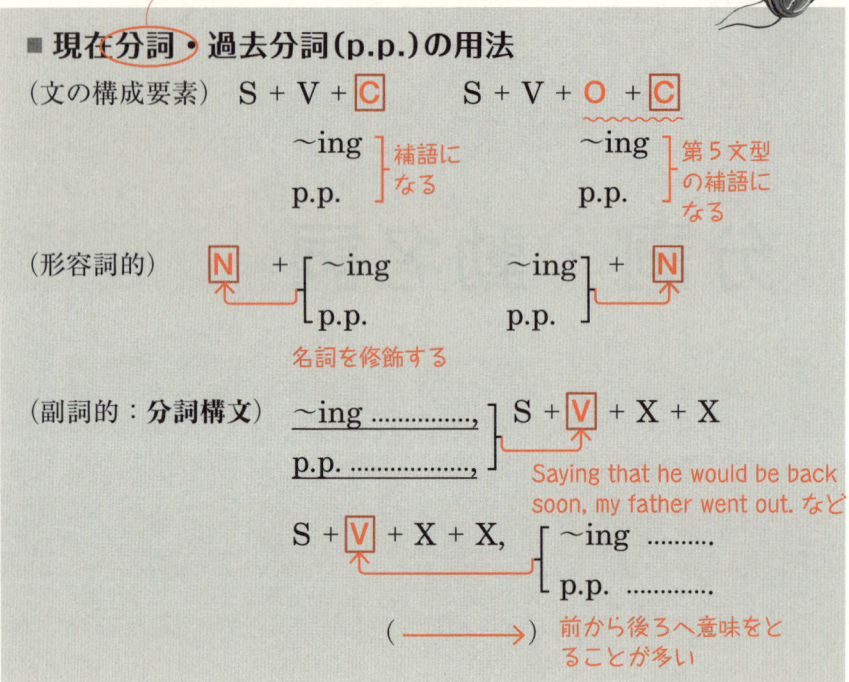

■ 現在分詞・過去分詞（p.p.）の用法

（文の構成要素）　S + V + C　　　S + V + O + C
　　　　　　　　　　～ing ｝補語に　　　～ing ｝第5文型
　　　　　　　　　　p.p.　 なる　　　　p.p.　　の補語になる

（形容詞的）　N + [～ing / p.p.]　　[～ing / p.p.] + N
　　　　　　　　　　名詞を修飾する

（副詞的：分詞構文）　[～ing……, / p.p.……,] S + V + X + X
　　　　　　　　　　　Saying that he would be back soon, my father went out. など

　　　　　　　　　　S + V + X + X, [～ing ……… / p.p. ………]

　　　　　　　　　　（→）前から後ろへ意味をとることが多い

1 次の英文中の（　）に入れるのに最も適当なものを選び，記号を○で囲みなさい。

ちかちか光る飛行物体が飛んで来るのを見た

(1) We saw a glimmering flying object (　　　) (toward us).
　　　S　V　　　　　　O　　　　　　　　　C　　私たちに向かって

　ア．to come　イ．coming　ウ．to coming　エ．to be coming

　● see + O + ～ing（…が～しているのを見る）→ "see + O + 原形不定詞" より情景がいきいきする
　● see + O + p.p.（…が～されるのを見る）
　　We saw it driven away.（それが追い払われるのを見た）
　　　　　　　destroyed.（それが破壊されるのを見た）　など

102

第9回　分詞・動名詞

(2) I don't think / I can make myself (　　　) in French.
　　　　　　　　　　　　 V'　　O'　　　C'
　　　　　　　　　　　　　　　　　　　　「私はフランス語で意思を
　　　　　　　　　　　　　　　　　　　　通じさせることはできない
×ア．understand　　　　㋑．understood　と思う」の意
　ウ．to understand　　　エ．to be understood

- **make oneself underspnderstood**（自分の考えが相手に理解されるようにする）
  　　　　　understand ではない　　→自分の考えを通じさせる
- S＋V＋O＋〜ing　「…が〜する」（能動）　｜
- S＋V＋O＋p.p.　 「…が〜される」（受動）　｝の意味が含まれる

　　　　　　いつ時計を修理してもらったのですか
(3) When did you have your watch (　　　)?
　　　　　　　　　　 V　　　O　　　　C

×ア．repair　イ．repairing　㋒．repaired　エ．to be repaired
　　　　　　　　　　　　　　「時計は修理される」だから p.p.

- 「…を〜させる，…を〜される，…を〜してもらう」
  S＋have＋O＋原形不定詞　「…が〜する」（能動）　｜
  S＋have＋O＋p.p.　　　「…が〜される」（受動）　｝の意味が含まれる
  　I had my kitten die.（子ネコを死なせた）
  　I had my watch stolen.（時計を盗まれた）

(4) He (　　　) by the car.
×ア．was killed his cat　　　イ．was his cat killed
　㋒．had his cat killed　　　エ．had his cat to be killed
　　　 V　 O　　C（過去分詞）
　　　　　「猫が殺される」（受動）だから p.p.

103

(5) ( ) the road, I missed my way. 　道を知らなかったので道に迷った
　㋐. Not knowing　　　×㋑. Knowing not
　㋒. For knowing not　　㋓. Not known

● 否定語の位置に注意！（〜ing の直前に置く）
As he was not familiar with the subject, he remained silent.
→ Being <u>not</u> familiar with …（×）
　 <u>Not</u> being familiar with …（○）

TRACK 02

名詞の働きをする。慣用的表現を正しく記憶しておく！

■ 動名詞の用法

（文の構成要素） S + V + X + X　　　　S + V + C
　　　　　　　　　〜ing　　　　　　　　　〜ing
　　　　　　　　文の主語になる　　　　　補語になる

　　　　　　　　S + V + O　　mind, enjoy, give up, avoid,
　　　　　　　　　　〜ing　　 finish, admit, stop　など
　　　　　　　　　　　　　　 不定詞ではなく動名詞を
　　　　　　　　　　　　　　 目的語にとる動詞

（前置詞 + 〜ing）
　in crossing the street（道路を渡る場合には）
　on hearing the news（ニュースを聞くとすぐに）　など

（その他：慣用的表現）以下の問題に多数含まれる

第9回　分詞・動名詞

(6) This book is really worth (　　) (more than once). 一度以上何度も
　　ア. reading　イ. being read　ウ. to read　エ. of reading
　　　　　　　　　　受動態にする必要はない

- (be) worth ～ing（～する価値がある）
- need ～ing, want ～ing（～する必要がある）
　　This PC needs repairing.
　　（このパソコンは修理が必要だ）

(7) I am looking forward (　　) your postcard from Alaska.
　　ア. receiving　×イ. to receive　ウ. to receiving　エ. in receiving
　　　　　　　　　　誤りやすい
　　　　　　　　　　I'm looking forward to see you.（×）
　　　　　　　　　　I'm looking forward to seeing you.（○）

- look forward to ～ing（～するのを楽しみに待つ）
　　不定詞ではなく動名詞（または名詞）
- with a view to ～ing（～する目的で）(for the purpose of ～ing)

(8) I am afraid that Tom will never succeed (　　) her love.
　　ア. winning　イ. to win　ウ. to winning　エ. in winning

- succeed in ～ing（～するのに成功する，見事に～する）
- fail in ～ing（～するのに失敗する）

(9) When Jane came, I had just finished (　　) the term paper.
　　(finish to write は×)
　　レポートを書き終えたところだった
　　ア. writing　イ. to write　ウ. to have written　エ. in writing
　　　　　　　　　×

105

- 不定詞ではなく動名詞を目的語とする動詞
  - mind ～ing（～するのを気にかける）
  - enjoy ～ing（～するのを楽しむ）
  - give up ～ing（～するのをやめる，あきらめる）
  - avoid ～ing（～するのを避ける） — She avoids meeting him.
  - finish ～ing（～し終わる）
  - admit ～ing（～したのを認める）
  - stop ～ing（～するのをやめる） ⎡ stop smoking（タバコをやめる，禁煙する）
                                  ⎣ stop to smoke（ちょっと一服する）

  He stopped thinking of her. ⎫
  He stopped to think of her. ⎬ 意味の違いは？
  （ちょっと考えた／ふと思いついた）
     （He paused to think of her.）
  He ceased to think her.（考えないようになった）

(10) Do you mind (　　　) the suitcase on this table?
　㋐ my putting　　　イ．for my putting
　ウ．me to put　　　エ．for me to put

- my ～ing（私が～すること）
- Do you mind ～ing …? / Do you mind if …? / ⎫
  Would you mind ～ing …? /   ⎬ （～しても
  Would you mind if … 過去形 …?   ⎭ かまいませんか）
                                                  応答にも注意！
  「私がスーツケースを置いてもかまいませんか」
  Do you mind if I put the suitcase …? ⎫
  Would you mind if I put the suitcase …? ⎬ 自然な言い方
     （過去形）

第9回　分詞・動名詞

> 「どうぞ，どうぞ」という返答は $\begin{cases} \text{Oh, certainly \underline{not}.} \\ \text{\underline{Not} at all.（ぜんぜんかまいません）} \end{cases}$
> 　　　　　　　　　　　　　　　　　　<u>否定</u>であることに注意！
> 「ちょっと困ります」なら Sorry, but <u>I'd rather you didn't</u> <u>if you don't mind</u>.
> 　　　　　　　　　　　　　　　　　そうしないでいただきたい　よろしかったら

〔解答〕
(1) イ　　(2) イ　　(3) ウ　　(4) ウ　　(5) ア
(6) ア　　(7) ウ　　(8) エ　　(9) ア　　(10) ア

TRACK 03

2 次の各組の(a)と(b)がほぼ同じ意味になるように，(b)の空所に1語ずつ入れなさい。

(1) (a) As I <u>had answered</u> the first question, I <u>began</u> to try the second.
　　　　　　過去完了　　　　　　　　　　　　　　　過去

(b) (Having) (answered) the first question, I began to try the second.

　　　Having failed three times, he never gave it up.

> ● having p.p. …（完了形の分詞構文）
> **not** having p.p. / **never** having p.p. → 否定語の位置にも注意
> (○) Never having read the book, …
> (×) Having never read the book, …
> 　　（その本を読んだことがなかったので…）

(2) (a) The matter <u>had been settled</u>, and the policemen <u>left</u> the scene.
　　　　　　　　過去完了　　　　　　　　　　　　　　　　　　過去

(b) The matter (settled), the policemen left the scene.
　　　　　　↑
　　　[having been]
　　　　省略

事がおさまったので現場を離れた

> ● S´ + (being / having been) + p.p.（受動態の分詞構文）
> 意味上の主語　　省略されるのが普通
> 　The quarrel settled, …（けんかがおさまったので…）
> 　This agreed, …（この事が合意されると…）
> →これらの形に慣れておくこと

第9回　分詞・動名詞

(3) (a) Tired and discouraged, I went to bed (earlier than usual).
　　　　↑Being は省略されるのが普通　　　　　　いつもより早く

　　(b) Since (I) (was) tired and discouraged, I went to bed earlier than usual.

> ● 形容詞..., S + V + X + X.
> ● 過去分詞..., S + V + X + X.
> 　　　分詞構文の形として慣れておく
> 　　　Hard of hearing, ...（耳が遠いので…）
> 　　　Seen from a distance, ...
> 　　　　（少し離れた所から見られると）

(4) (a) I heard someone singing an American folk song.
　　　　　V　　　O　　　　C

　　(b) I heard an American folk song (sung) (by) someone.
　　　　　V　　　　　O　　　　　　　　　　C↑
　　　　　　　（歌がうたわれる）　　　　sing ― sang ―(sung)

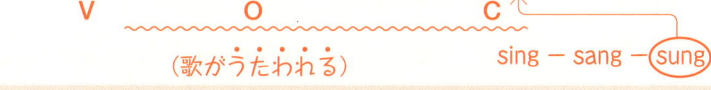

> ● hear + O +原形 / ～ing（…が～するのを聞く）
> ● hear + O + p.p.（…が～されるのを聞く）
> 　　　↑ここに「…が～される」の意味が含まれている

(5) (a) I remember / that I saw her somewhere two or three times.

　　(b) I remember (seeing) (her) somewhere two or three times.

> ● remember ～ing（[過去に]～したのを覚えている）
> 　 remember to ～（[これから]～するのを忘れていない）　区別する
> 　　　　　　　　　I remember to see her tomorrow.
> ● その他 forget, try, like, start, ...
> 　 try to ～（～しようとする）　　like to ～（[今]～したいと思う）
> 　 try ～ing（試しに～してみる）　like ～ing（～するのが好き）

109

(6) (a) There is no hope that he will be saved.
　　(b) There is no hope of (his[him]) (being) saved.
　　　　彼が救われる見込みはない

> - **I don't like your[you] going out alone at night.**
>   I don't like my son[my son's] going out ...
>   I'm convinced of the report being mistaken.
>   　　報告が間違っている(と確信している)
> - 意味上の主語は？　→　代名詞なら所有格[または目的格]
>   　　　　　　　　　　　名詞なら目的格[または所有格]

(7) (a) It is impossible / to know what will happen to us next year.
　　　　　～するのは不可能だ
　　(b) There is (no) (knowing) what will happen to us next year.
　　　　　来年に何が起こるかわからない

> - **There is no ～ing.（～することはできない）という形**
>   (It is very difficult to ～. / One cannot ～.)

　　　　いつ…しても／…するたびに　　　　故郷を思い出す
(8) (a) Whenever I see this picture, I think of my hometown.
　　(b) I cannot see this picture (without) (thinking) of my hometown.
　　　　　　　　　　　思い出さずに見ることはできない[二重否定]
　　　　　　　　　　　→見れば必ず思い出す[肯定]

> - **cannot ... without ～ing（…すれば必ず～する）**
> - その他，動名詞を含む語句
>   **feel like ～ing**（～したい気がする）
>   **on ～ing**（～するとすぐに）

> **object to ~ing**（～することに反対する）
>   I have no objection to ~ing.（～するのに異議はない）
> **of one's own ~ing**（自分で～した…）
>   a picture of his own painting　（彼が自分で描いた絵）
>   a book ⎡ of my (own) choosing
>   ⎣ of my (own) choice
>   （自分で選んだ書物）

〔解答〕
(1) **Having answered** the first question, I began to try the second.
(2) The matter **settled**, the policeman left the scene.
(3) Since **I was** tired and discouraged, I went to bed earlier than usual.
(4) I heard an American folk song **sung by** someone.
(5) I remember **seeing her** somewhere two or three times.
(6) There is no hope of **his being** saved.
(7) There is **no knowing** what will happen to us next year.
(8) I cannot see this picture **without thinking** of my hometown.

3 次の日本文を英語に直しなさい。(1)〜(3)は(　)内の語のうち最も適当なものを選んで使用すること。

(1) 台所には牛乳が何本か残っています。

(leave, leaving, left)

Some bottles of milk are left in the kitchen.

→ There are some bottles of milk left in the kitchen.
　　　　　　V　　　　S

(There を文頭にしたときの語順に注意)

- **there is ... ~ing**

    Weeds are springing up ...

    → There are weeds springing up ...

    (…に雑草が生えてきている)

- **there is ... p.p.**

    Some sugar is left in the cupboard.

    → There is some sugar left ...

    (食器戸棚の中に砂糖がいくらか残っている)

(2) 私は作文をスミスさんに訂正してもらいたいと思っています。

(correct, collecting, corrected)

I want / I'd like] Mr. Smith to correct my composition.

→ I want / I'd like] my composition corrected by Mr. Smith.
　　　　　　　　　　O　　　　　　C　　作文が訂正される

- want + O + to ~ / I'd like ... to ~（…に~してもらいたいと思う）
  want + O + p.p. / I'd like ... p.p.（…が~されるように望んでいる）
  I want my trousers ironed.
  （ズボンにアイロンをかけてもらいたい）

- have + O + 原形, have + O + p.p.（…に~させる，…に~してもらう）
  （参考）
  I want to have Mr. Smith correct my composition.
  I want to have my composition corrected by Mr. Smith.

(3) 両親は妹が１人で旅行に行くのに反対しています。
　　alone, by herself／go on a trip／be against ~ing
(for, against, with)

My parents are against my sister's[my sister] going on a trip by herself.

- be against ~（~に反対している）
  be for ~（~に賛成している）
    コーヒー飲まない？ — I'm all for that.（大賛成だよ）
- my sister's ~ing / my sister ~ing（妹が~すること）
    所有格　　　　目的格
  （意味上の主語）

(4) ［晴れた日にはこの芝生の上に寝ころんで，］［(青空に浮かんでいる)雲を眺めながら，］私たちはいろいろなことを語り合ったものでした。

on fine days / lie on the grass / talk with each other / used to ～ / would often ～

<u>Lying down on this grass on fine days, we used to talk about a lot of things with each other, looking at the clouds floating across[in] the blue sky.</u>
（lie の現在分詞）

- ～ing ………, S + V + X + X, ～ing ……….
  （分詞構文）　　　主文　　　（分詞構文）

〔解答〕
(1) **There are some bottles of milk left in the kitchen.**
(2) **I want (to have) my composition corrected by Mr. Smith.**
(3) **My parents are against my sister('s) going on a trip by herself.**
(4) **Lying down on this grass on fine days, we used to talk a lot to[with] each other, looking at the clouds floating across the blue sky.**

第 10 回

名詞・代名詞・冠詞

TRACK 01

■ 数の概念など

日本語：単数・複数をあまり区別しない
　　　　名詞・代名詞の格変化はない　…私 ─┬ は／が／の
　　　　　（助詞で表す）　　　　　　　　　├ に／へ
　　　　　　　　　　　　　　　　　　　　 └ を

英　語：<u>単数・複数</u>を必ず区別する ◎
　　　　冠詞の有無には<u>必ず注意する</u>
　　　　名詞・代名詞に<u>格変化がある</u>… I, my, me, mine, myself
　　　　　（主格・所有格・目的格）　　　 you, your, you,
　　　　　　　　　　　　　　　　　　　　 yourself, yourselves

　　　　　　　　　　　　　　　　　　　　　　　　　　など

1 次の英文中には不適当な語が1つずつ含まれています。その語に下線を引き，正しい形に直しなさい。

　　　　　　　　　　　　　たくさんの情報　　　　　奨学金について
(1) Mr. Brown gave us a lot of <u>informations</u> (about scholarship).
　　　　　　　　　　　　　　　　　　×　　　　　　（ information ）

> ● 単数か複数か？　数か量か？
> informátion（情報），advíce（忠告）（advise と区別），
> évidence（証拠），…　　　複数形にしない名詞
> 　　　　　　　　　　　　　　　　some advice（○）
> 　　　　　　　　　　　　　　　　some advices（×）
> 　　　　　　　　　　　　　　　　a piece of advice（○）
> a piece of ～（1つの～），two pieces of ～（2つの～）

116

第10回　名詞・代名詞・冠詞

(2) The bill met strong objéct (from the opposition parties).
　　　法案　　　　強い反対に遭った　　　野党から　　(objection)

- 紛らわしい名詞の区別。
  - óbject（目的，対象）
  - objéction（異議，反対）(object の名詞形)
  - obsérvance（[規則などを]守ること）
  - observátion（観察）　　　　　　} obsérve の名詞形
  - discóvery（発見）
  - invéntion（発明）
  - evolútion（進化）(evolve の名詞形)
      the theory of evolution（進化論）
  - revolútion（革命），その他

(3) The burglar crawled (into the room) (on all four).
　　　　　　　　　這って侵入した　　　　　　四つん這いで
　　強盗，住居侵入者　　　　　　　　　　　　　　　　(fours)

- on one's knees（ひざをついて）
- on one foot（片足で）　　stand on one's feet（自分の足で立つ→独立する）

(4) [When the boy was called by name], he jumped to his foot.
　　　　　　　　　　call ... by name（…の名を呼ぶ）　ぱっと跳び上がった
　　　　　　　　　　　　　　　　　　　　　　　　　　　　(feet)

- jump to one's feet（跳び上がる）
  └ foot（足）（単数形）の複数形

117

(5) My uncle comes to see us every two week.
　　　　　　　　　　　　　　　　　　　　×　　　(weeks)

- every ~, every two ~s
  通例は単数形の名詞
  two weeks（2週間ごとに）
  three years（3年ごとに）
  など複数形を置ける。

TRACK 02

　　　　　　　　　　　　　　　　婦人用下着類
(6) Mrs. Smith bought some ladie's underwear for her daughters.
　　　　　　　　　　　　　　　　×　　　　○　　(ladies')
　　　　　　　　　　　　　　　　　　　　　　　　sの後にアポストロフィ

- únderwear（下着類），fúrniture（家具類），machínery（機械[装置]）　複数形にしない名詞
- 複数名詞の所有格は？
  { two minute's walk（×）
  { two minutes' walk（○）「歩いて2分間の距離」
  lady〈単数〉→ ladies〈複数〉→ ladies'〈所有格〉
  「婦人物売り場」は the ladies' corner department counter

　　　　　　　　　　　　　　　　　　　　　　夫の好み
　　　　　　　　　　　　　　　　　　　　　（よりすぐれている）
(7) Sarah's taste for clothing is better than her husband.
　　　　衣類の好み　　　　　　　　　　　　　　×
　　　　　　　　　　　　　　　　　　　　　(husband's)

- 何と何を比較しているのか？
  → Sarah's taste と her husband's (taste) を比較

第10回　名詞・代名詞・冠詞

(8) <u>Three of us</u> — <u>Nancy, Helen and me</u> — decided to join the
　　　S　　　　　　　　　　　　　×
　　　　　　　　　　　主語(S)と同格だから　　　テニスクラブに入ろうと決めた
　　　　　　　　　　　me(目的格)→ I(主格)
tennis club.　　　　　　　　　　　　　　　　　　　　　　(I)

- 主格―所有格―目的格

(9) Mathematics is <u>one of Ben's favorite subject</u>.
　　　　　　　　　　　　　　　　　　　　　×
　　　　数学はベンの得意科目の1つだ　　　　　　　(subjects)

- **one of the ～s**（～のうち 1 人[1 つ]）
　　　　　　　複数名詞
　　one of the boys
　　one of the towns　　}などに慣れておく
　　one of the countries

(10) Nobody could speak to Andy. He was beside <u>oneself</u> (with
　　　　　　　　　　　　　　　　　　　　　　　　　　×
anger).　　　　　　　　　　　　　　　我を忘れていた
怒りで　　　　　　　　　　　　　　　　　　　　(himself)

- **oneself** → **myself, yourself, yourselves, himself, herself,
　　ourselves, themselves** などになる

119

■ 前置詞＋oneself

be beside oneself with (anger（［怒りで］逆上している）
                         joy（［喜んで］有頂天になっている）

by oneself
- 「ひとりぼっちで」（alone）　She lives by herself.
- 「独力で」　She did it by herself.

for oneself（独力で，自分自身のために）
　She kept it for herself.（自分のためにとっておいた）
　She did it for herself.（自分でやった）

of itself（自然に，ひとりでに）

have ～ to oneself（～を自分専用にする）
　I have a room to myself.

keep ～ to oneself（自分の心にしまっておく）
　keep it to yourself

〔解答〕
(1) informations → information　　(2) object → objection
(3) four → fours　　(4) foot → feet
(5) week → weeks　　(6) ladie's → ladies'
(7) husband → husband's　　(8) me → I
(9) subject → subjects　　(10) oneself → himself

第10回 名詞・代名詞・冠詞

■ 冠詞の有無，a と the の区別

2 次の英文中の空所に適当な冠詞を入れなさい。ただし，入れる必要がない場合は×を記入しなさい。

(1) You must take (the) medicine (three times (a) day).
  （その）薬　　　　　　　　1日に3回
  　　　　　　　　　　　　　　　　　～につき (per)

- twice a week（1週間に2度）
  three times a month（1か月に3回）

(2) I want you to be (a) Newton, [not (a) Shakespeare].
  　　　　　　　　～のような人　　Shakespeare のような人ではなく

- a / an ＋固有名詞
  Newton と a Newton (a scientist like Newton)
  Shakespeare と a Shakespeare (a dramatist like Shakespeare)
  Mozart と a Mozart (a composer like Mozart) など。

(3) Bill patted me on (the) shoulder / and asked me what I had
  　　　　私の肩を叩いた

  been doing (in (the) afternoon).
  　　　　　　　午後に

- pat ... on the shoulder（…の肩を叩く）
  strike ... on the head（…の頭を叩く）
  grasp ... by the hand（…の手を固く握る）

121

- in the afternoon（午後に）
  in the morning（午前に）
- at noon（正午に）
  at night（夜に） ｝冠詞はつけないのが慣用
- in the evening（夕方に，晩に）

(4) (In Japan) workers are paid by (the) month, / while (in Britain) by (the) week.

　　workers are paid が省略
　　by (the) month → 1か月単位で，月給で
　　by (the) week → 1週単位で，週給で
　　while → 一方…では

- by the month（月単位で）
- by the hour（時間単位で）
  hire a boat by the hour（ボートを1時間いくらで借りる）
- by the pound（ポンド単位で）…
  be sold by the pound（1ポンドいくらで売られる）

(5) Airplane travel is becoming incréasingly pópular, / but travel by (×) car is (by far) (the) commonest.

　　ますます人気が出ている
　　車での旅（車を使っての旅）
　　断然（最も）普通　飛び抜けてあたりまえ

- by car, by bus, by train
- by airplane, by air（空路で）
  by boat, by sea（船で）
  by land（陸路で）

122

> - be hit by <u>a bus</u>　　The cat was hit ┌ by bus.（×）
> 　　　　　　　　　　　　　　　　　　　　 └ by a bus.（○）

　　　　　　　　　　　とてもおかしい話をしたので…
(6) Peter told us (×) <u>such (a) funny story</u> / that we all <u>burst into (×) laughter</u>.
　　　　　　　　　　　　　　　　　この語順

> - such a funny story ┐
>   so funny a story   ├ 語順に注意すること◎
>   too funny a story ┘
> - burst into laughter（どっと笑う）
>   burst into tears（急に泣き出す）

(7) (×) <u>most</u> people said / that they had <u>never</u> known <u>so (×) hot (a) summer</u>.
　　　　　　　　　　　　　　　　　こんなに暑い夏は初めてだ

> - most ～s / most of the ～s（たいていの～，～の大部分）
>   most people / most of the people（たいていの人たち）
> - such a ～
>   such a hot summer
> - so ＋形容詞＋ a ＋名詞 (as ～)
>   so hot a summer（語順に注意）
> - as ＋形容詞＋ a ＋名詞 (as ～)
>   as hot a summer (as last year)

> - **too** ＋形容詞＋ a ＋名詞 (to ～)
>   too hot a summer for us to stay in Tokyo
>   （私たちが東京にいるには暑すぎる夏）

(8) Fred had to pay (×) double (the) usual price.
　　　　　　　　　　　　　通常の値段の2倍

> - **double the ～**（～の倍）
>   drive at double the usual speed（いつもの倍のスピードで）
>   He earns double my salary.
>   　　　　　私の給料の倍
> - **twice the length of ～**
> - **twice as long as ～**　 }（～の2倍長い）

〔解答〕
(1) the, a　(2) a, a　(3) the, the　(4) the, the　(5) ×, the
(6) ×, a, ×　(7) ×, ×, a　(8) ×, the

第10回 名詞・代名詞・冠詞

TRACK 04

■ 代名詞の用法

- one と ones, one と it
- it と that, that と those
- both と all, both と either
- either と neither, neither と none
- the other と another, some と others

([2つの]いずれも…でない)
区別する。
([3つ以上の]いずれも…でない)

（2つのうちのもう1つ）　（多くのうちのもう1つ）

---

3 下の文中の空所に入れるのに最も適当な語を(a)〜(n)から選びなさい。

(a) one　(b) ones　(c) it　(d) that　(e) those
(f) both　(g) all　(h) either　(i) neither　(j) none
(k) other　(l) the other　(m) another　(n) others

(1) Dennis came in. His hands were (both) dirty with mud.
　　　　　　　　　　　　　手は‥‥‥‥‥ 両方とも　　泥で汚れていた

(2) It is one thing to make a plan, / and (another) to carry it out.
　　　　　　計画を立てる　　　[it is]　　　　　実行する

- **A is one thing and B is another.**（A と B とは別だ）
　　　　　　　　　　　（A とは）別のこと

(3) I like fishing. I have a new fishing rod and several old (**ones**).
釣り竿　　　　　　　　　　　(fishing rods)

- **several old ones, some blue ones**
  I don't like this color. Could you show me some blue ones?

(4) The beer of Germany is said to be stronger than (**that**)
ドイツのビール　　　　　　　　　　　　　　　　　　　(= the beer)
of our country.　　　　　　　　　　　　　　　　　日本のビール

- **that of ～**（単数名詞を比べる場合）
- **those of ～**（複数名詞を比べる場合）
  These apples are better than those in the box.

(5) The meeting had to be held (with only (**those**) present).

出席していた人たち
those (who were) present

- **those (people who are) present**
  those wounded（負傷した人たち）
  those standing（立っている人たち）

2人のうちどちらも正しくなかった
(6) Two students answered the question, / but (**neither**) of them
was right.　2人の学生が答えたけれども

(only) one　◯
either　△ ── 文脈から neither
both　×　　　のほう
none　×

- **neither**（2人, 2つについて使う）か **none**（3つ以上に使う）か？

第10回　名詞・代名詞・冠詞

(7) Betty bought two fashionable ties. One was for her father and (the other) was for her boyfriend.

流行の, いきな
2つのうち片方は父親用, もう片方は恋人用

- the other(the + other)とanother(an + other)の区別

(8) Lucy has not been ill for a long time, and she has forgotten what (it) is like / to be confined to bed (for some days).

to ～がどういうものなのか　　何日間も病床につくこと

- what it is like / to ～　　itは形式主語でto ～をうける

(9) Bill wants a portable word processor, / but he cannot afford to buy (one).

～する余裕がない
a portable word processor
(the ではない)

- one ← a ＋名詞
- it ← the ＋名詞

He has a car. He likes driving it.
(one ではない)

(10) Some of my father's golf clubs are imported ones / and (others) homemade.

輸入品
[are]

- some ... others ～（あるものは…またあるものは～, …もあれば～もある）
  Some say this and others say that.
  （こう言う者もいればああ言う者もいる）

127

〔解答〕
(1) (f)　(2) (m)　(3) (b)　(4) (d)　(5) (e)
(6) (i)　(7) (l)　(8) (c)　(9) (a)　(10) (n)

TRACK 05

■ 会話の慣用表現

4 日本語を参考にして，英文中の空所を完成させなさい。

(1) 「鉛筆と紙を使っていいですか」「いいですよ。はいどうぞ」
　　Can I use a pencil and some paper? —— Yes, of course. Here (you) (are).

> ● **Here you are.**（「はい，どうぞ」と差し出すときの慣用表現）
> 　Do you have a pen? — Yes, here you are.

(2) 「ここはどこですか」「もうじき新宿です」
　　Where (is) (this)? —— We're coming to Shinjuku in a minute.
　　　　　└ (here は×)
　　　　　　(here は副詞だから主語には使わない)

> ● Where is this?　⎫
> 　Where am I?　　 ⎬ 「ここはどこ？」
> 　Where are we?　⎭
> ● (This)(place) is ...　「ここは禁煙室だ」This is a nonsmoking room.
> ● (Here) is ...　⎫
> 　Here are ...s.　⎬ 「ここに…がある」

第 10 回　名詞・代名詞・冠詞

(3)「試験に失敗したんだってね」「しかたないさ。ひどいカゼをひいていたんだから」

You failed the exam, didn't you? ── I couldn't (help) (it). I had a terrible cold.

(failed the exam → flunked the exam)
(help:「助ける」ではなく「避ける」という感じ)

- I cannot help it.
  It cannot be helped. 〉（しかたがない, どうしようもない）
- Help yourself, please.（どうぞご自由に取って食べてください）

〔解答〕
(1) Yes, of course. Here you are.
(2) Where is this?/ Where am I?/ Where are we?
(3) I couldn't help it. I had a terrible cold.

TRACK 06

5 次の日本文を英語に直しなさい。ただし，（ ）内の語を用いること。

(1) (あそこに見える)建物が女子学生の寮ですよ。(dormitory)

口語では dorm

The building (that) you can see over there is the women students'[girl students' / female students'] dormitory.

スペリングに注意
student's (×)
students' (○)

- **a woman student**
  a woman doctor 〉の複数形は？ → women students / women doctors (女性医師)

  スペリングに注意。girl's (×), girls' (○)
- **a girls' dormitory**
  a women's dormitory 〉「女子寮」
  a coeds' dorm ([男女共学の]女子学生寮)

(2) 彼のような才能の持ち主があの若さで死んだとは, / かえすがえすも残念なことです。(it)

　　a man of his talent　　　　He died so young. ("he = so young" で死んだ)
　　　　　　　　　　　　　　S　V　　C

　it is a pity that ... (should) ~

It is a great pity / that a man of his talent [died / should have died] so young.

- **a man of his talent / a talented man like him**
  　a man of his ability
  　a man of his age
- **it is a pity that ... (should) ~**

〔解答〕

(1) The building you can see over there is the dormitory for women students.

(2) It is a great pity that a man of his talent should have died so young. / It is a matter of great regret that a talented man like him died so young.

第11回

形容詞・副詞・疑問詞

■ 形容詞・副詞

（文の構成要素）　S + V + [C]　　S + V + O + [C]
　　　　　　　　　　　　　Adj.　　　　　　　　Adj.

第2文型の補語・第5文型の補語に形容詞が使われる

（形容詞・副詞の修飾関係）

Adj. + [N]　　　　　　[N] + Adj.

形容詞は名詞を修飾する

Adv.　[S + V + X + X]　　S + [V] + X + X
　　　　　　（文）　　　　　　　Adv.

副詞は主に動詞を修飾する
He works very hard.

Adv. + [Adj./Adv.]

[Adj./Adv.] + Adv.

形容詞・副詞を修飾することもある
very hard, kind enough

---

1 次の英文中の下線部(a)(b)のうち，どちらか一方は不適当です。例にならって，誤っている語を正しい形に直しなさい。

(例)　Helen and Jane look very (a)much (b)like. (SVC)

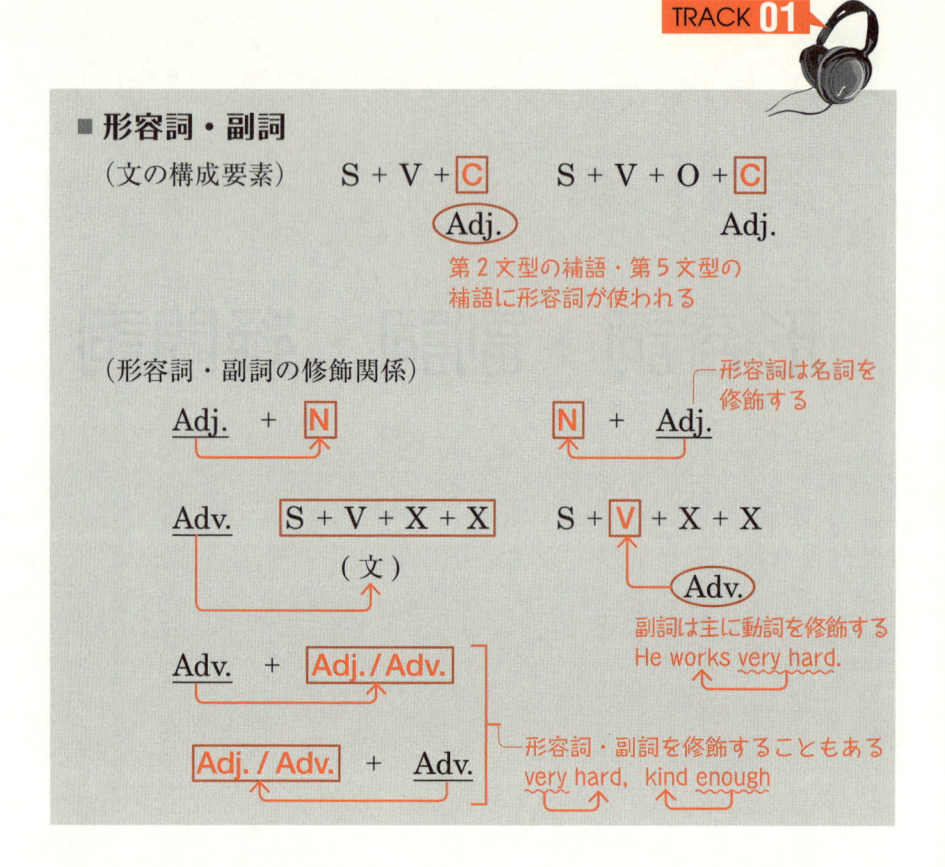

(答)　(b) alike
「お互いに似ている」という形容詞

「〜と似ている」
They look like.(×)
They look like each other.(○)
（お互い相手と似ている）

134

第 11 回　形容詞・副詞・疑問詞

- very と much / late と latter / hard と hardly
  also, too と not ... either / many と much / few と a few /
  before と ago　などを区別する

(1) I'm feeling (a)very better than (b)yesterday.
　　　　　　　　○ much　　　昨日より体の調子がずっと良い

- **much better**（much は比較級を強める）
  very well（原級を強めるのは very）
- **much the best / the very best**（最上級を強める）
  ほかに by far the best（ずばぬけて最上）

(2) The (a)later half of this detective story is (b)quite interesting.
　　　　○ latter　　この探偵小説の後半部はとてもおもしろい

- late－later－latest　　時間的に「遅い，遅く」
  late－latter－last　　順序について使う
  　the latter half（後半部），the last ～（最後の～）

(3) Bill works very (a)hardly (every day (b)of the week).
　　　　　　　　　○ hard　　週の毎日，とてもよく働く［勉強する］

- **hard**（いっしょうけんめい）
- **hardly**（ほとんど～でない）
  He hardly works.（彼はほとんど働かない）

135

- **scarcely**（ほとんど〜でない）
- **seldom / rarely**（めったに〜しない）

(4) [If your sons don't go to see the circus,] (a)<u>mine</u> won't, (b)<u>too</u>.
　　　　　　　　　　　　　　　　　　　　　うちの息子も行かない
　　　　　　　　　　　　　　　　　　　　　(my sons)
○ either

- **too, also**（〜もまた）〈肯定文で〉
- **not ... either**（〜もまた…でない）〈否定文で〉

　　{ If you go, I will, too.
　　 If you don't go, I won't, either.

(5) (Last year) there (a)<u>were</u> not (b)<u>much</u> earthquakes (in Japan).
　　　　　　　　　　　　　　　　○ many　多くの地震があった

- **many 〜s**　←数が多い
- **much 〜**　←量が多い

(6) Isabel said / that she had arrived there a (a)<u>few</u> days (b)<u>ago</u>.
　　　　　　　　　　　　　　　　　　　　2, 3日前に着いたと言った
　　　　　　　　　　　　　　　　　　　　（言ったときより）
○ before

　　　　　　　　　　　I arrived here { a few days ago.（○）
　　　　　　　　　　　　　　　　　　 a few days before.（×）

- **ago**（[今から] 〜前に）
- **before**（[過去（や未来）のある時から] 〜前に）

第11回　形容詞・副詞・疑問詞

(7) Can you imagine / (a)how (b)beautifully the mountains look (at sunset)?

　　　　　　　　　　　　　　　　×　山々がどんなに美しく見えるか
　　　　　　　　　　　　　　　　○ beautiful
　V′　　　　日没に　　　　　　　　C′(形容詞)　　S′

- S + V + Ⓒ ← SVC の C が形容詞 (副詞ではない)
  The mountains { are beautiful.
  　　　　　　　　look beautiful.
  　　　　　　　　(beautifully は×)

- look + Adj.
  You look pale.
  You look happy. など

- feel + Adj.
  He was ill.
  He felt ill.　(he = ill)

- S + V + O + Adj.
  push the door open
  (押して"窓 = open"の状態にする) → 窓を押し開ける

(8) The trouble was / that his house was (a)rather too
　　　　　　×　困ったことに…
(b)narrow (for his family).
　○ small

- wide（幅が広い）と large（面積が広い）
- narrow（幅が狭い）と small（大きさが狭い）

137

- thick（濃い）と thin（うすい）
  strong（[コーヒー・茶が]濃い）と weak（[コーヒー・茶が]うすい）
  long（[鼻が]高い）と short（[鼻が]低い）
- その他「人々が多い(少ない)」は a large [small] population
  （many, few は×）

(9) Our coach wanted us all to become (a)possible× to swim (b)faster.　私たち全員が～できるようになるのを望んだ　○ able

- able と possible
  人が主語　　人を主語にするのは不可！
- be able to ～（～できる）　I'm able to do it.
  be capable of ～ing（～する能力がある）　I'm capable of doing it.
- it is possible for ... to ～（…が～できる）
    It's possible for me to do it.

(10) You should be (a)respectable× (toward your (b)elders).
　　　　　　　　　○ respectful　　　年長者には敬意をこめて
　　　　　　　　　　　　　　　　　丁重にすべきだ

- respéctable（まあまあの, 見苦しくない, まあまともな）
- respéctful（[人が]丁重な）
- respéctive（それぞれの）
    their respective countries
    respect は「点」の意
    in this respect(この点では), in no respect(どの点でも…ない)
- imáginative（想像力のある）, imáginary（想像上の）

138

〔解答〕
(1) (a) much   (2) (a) latter   (3) (a) hard   (4) (b) either
(5) (b) many   (6) (b) before   (7) (b) beautiful   (8) (b) small
(9) (a) able   (10) (a) respectful

2 次の(a), (b)の2文がほぼ同じ意味になるように，空所に適当な1語を入れなさい。

(1) (a) My uncle kindly gave me one of his coins.
(b) My uncle was kind (enough) to give me one of his coins.
（親切にも～してくれた）

- be kind enough to ～
- be so kind as to ～ （～するくらい親切だ）⇒親切にも～してくれる
- have the kindness to ～ （～する親切心がある）

(2) (a) Catherine plays golf very well.
(b) Catherine is very (good) at playing golf.
　　　　S　　V　　C

- well（うまく[副詞]），good（うまい[形容詞]）
- be good at ～（～するのがうまい）

(3) (a) Mrs. Baker takes great pride in her son Dick.
(b) Mrs. Baker is very (proud) of her son Dick.
（～を誇りにしている）

- pride（誇り[名詞]），proud（誇りに思う[形容詞]）

第11回　形容詞・副詞・疑問詞

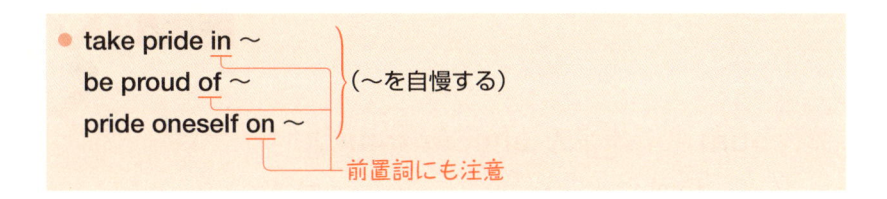

- take pride in 〜
- be proud of 〜 　（〜を自慢する）
- pride oneself on 〜
　　　　　　　　　前置詞にも注意

　　　　　　　　　　　　　　赤ちゃんの面倒を見るのに
(4) (a) You should be very careful (in looking after the baby).
　　　　　　　　　　　　　　　　　　　　　　　　　　　(SVC)

　(b) You should look after the baby very (carefully).
　　　　　　　　〜を世話する　　　　　　　　　　　　　(SVO)

- careful［形容詞］と carefully［副詞］

　　　　　　　　　　　　　どろぼうが逮捕されなかったのは…
(5) (a) It was unfórtunate / that the robber was not arrésted.

　(b) (Unfortunately) the robber was not arrested.
　　　（不幸にも，不幸なことに）　文全体を修飾する

- 文全体を修飾する副詞
　fórtunately, luckily（幸運にも）
　unfórtunately, unluckily（不幸にも）
　naturally（当然のことながら，もちろん）

　He died miserably.
　（みじめな死に方をした）
　Miserably he died.
　（みじめにも死んでしまった）

- fortune（財産，［幸］運）
　misfórtune（不運）
　　　　　　　　　名詞の接頭辞にも注意（un- ではない）

〔解答〕
(1) **enough**　(2) **good**　(3) **proud**　(4) **carefully**　(5) **Unfortunately**

TRACK 04

■ countable C と uncountable U

few – fewer – fewest
many – more – most } + C — countable 数えられる名詞に使う

little – less – least
much – more – most } + U — uncountable 数えられない名詞に使う

3 次の文中の空所に few, little, many, much の適当な形を入れなさい。必要な場合には比較級・最上級に変化させること。

今ではインディアンの数が少なくなっていると・

Many people think / that there are (1)(**fewer**) Indians now
　　　　　　　　　　　　　　　　　　　　　［数が］少ない

[than when the white settlers first came to America], / but I
　　　　　　　　　　白人の入植者たち

have read / that there are more. They have, (however),

(2)(**less**) land (than they used to) / and cannot live (by
　［量が］少ない　　以前より　　　　［have］　狩猟では生きられない

hunting and fishing).

● fewer Indians （アメリカ・インディアンの数が以前より少ない）
● less land （土地が以前より少ない）

There is much poverty and much illness (among the
Indians).
　　　　　　　|
　　　(many ではない)　　　貧困と病がインディアンの間に広がっている

第11回 形容詞・副詞・疑問詞

The (3)(**more**) white settlers came, / the **more** land they took (from Indians). There are not (4)(**many**) jobs for them (when they do not have (5)(**much**) education).

> - **the more ..., the more 〜**（…すればするほど[その分だけ]ますます〜）
>   Many white settlers came → The more white settlers came
>   they took much land → the more land they took
>   「多くの白人入植者が来れば来るほど，それだけますます多くの土地を奪った」
> - **many jobs**（多くの仕事）
> - **much education**（十分な教育）
>   「あまり教育を受けてない場合には仕事もあまりない」の意

There are schools (on the reservátions). But (6)(**few**) go to high school and (7)(**fewer**) to college (because they do not have money enough).

(注) reservátion「（インディアンのための）特別保留地」
「特別保留地に学校はあるものの，高校へ行くインディアンは少なく，大学となるともっと少数しか行かない」

> - その他
>   **a lot of, lots of**（多数の，多量の）── a lot of people / a lot of money / lots of presents　など
>   **a large number of**（多数の）

a good[great] deal of（多量の）── a good deal of { water / snow / ice }　など

plenty of（十分な，たっぷりの）── plenty of { books / time }　など

〔解答〕
(1) **fewer**　(2) **less**　(3) **more**　(4) **many**
(5) **much**　(6) **few**　(7) **fewer**

第11回　形容詞・副詞・疑問詞

TRACK 05

■ 疑問詞
　　　　　　　　　┌─形容詞・副詞とともに使える
who, what, which, how, why, where, when
　　　　　　　　What do you think of it?　┐
　　　　　　　　How do you like it?　　　┘ how と what を区別

4 [　]内の日本語を参考にして，次の英文中の空所に適当な語を入れなさい。

(1) How (often) were you absent from school?　［何回］
　　　(How many times)　　　　　　　　　　　　返答は Oh, not very often. /
　　　　　　　　　　　　　　　　　　　　　　　Three times a week. など

　● **How often ...? / How many times ...?**（何回…か）
　　日本へは何回目？　How many times have you been here?

(2) How (far) is it from here to your father's office?
　　　　　　　　　　　　　　　　　　　　［距離はどのくらい］
　　返答は It's only [just] five minutes' walk. など

　● **How far is it from A to B?**（A から B まで距離はどのくらいか）

(3) How (long) has he been ill in bed?　［いつから］
　　　返答は He's been ill ┌ for more than a month.
　　　　　　　　　　　　　└ since last year.　　　　　など

> ● How long …?（どのくらいの期間…か，いつから…，いつまで…）
> How long have you been here?
> How long are you going to stay here?

┌─ 〜する余裕がある

(4) How (much) can you afford?　[金額はいくら]「いくら出せる？」
返答は Not very much. I'm afraid I can afford only five dollars.
「あんまり（出せないな）。たったの5ドルくらい（なら出せるんじゃない）かな」

> ● How much …?
> How much is this?（これいくら？）（What's the price of this?）
> How much does it cost?（それいくら？）（What is its price?）

(5) How (soon) will this be ready?　[いつごろまでに]
返答は Well, it'll be ready in two days.
「いつごろ[用意が]できますか？」「あと2日でできますよ」

> ● How soon …?（あとどのくらいしたら…？）
> How soon is your school starting?（いつ始まるの？）
> How soon is our train leaving?（あとどのくらいで出るの？）

(6) How (often) do the trains run?　[何分おきに]
返答は Every twenty minutes.
「列車は何分おきに出ますか？」「20分おきに出ます」

〔解答〕
　(1) often　(2) far　(3) long　(4) much　(5) soon　(6) often

第11回　形容詞・副詞・疑問詞

5 次のAとBの会話を英語に直しなさい。

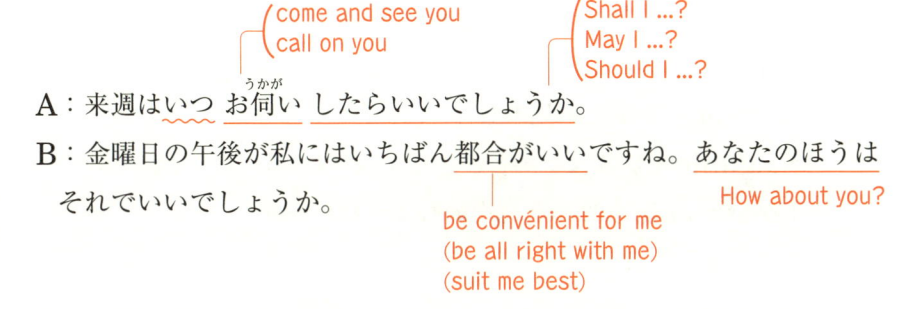

A：来週はいつ お伺い したらいいでしょうか。
（お伺い → come and see you / call on you）
（したらいい → Shall I ...? / May I ...? / Should I ...?）

B：金曜日の午後が私にはいちばん都合がいいですね。あなたのほうはそれでいいでしょうか。
（都合がいい → be convénient for me / (be all right with me) / (suit me best)）
（あなたのほうは → How about you?）

A：What time shall I come and see you next week?

- **When ...?**（いつ…か）
- **What time ...?**（いつ，何時に…か）
- **Which day ...?**（どの日に…か）
  「何曜日がいいですか？」
  Which day (of the week) will it be convénient for you?

B：Friday afternoon will[would] be most convenient for me. Will that suit you? [How about you? / Would it be all right with you?]

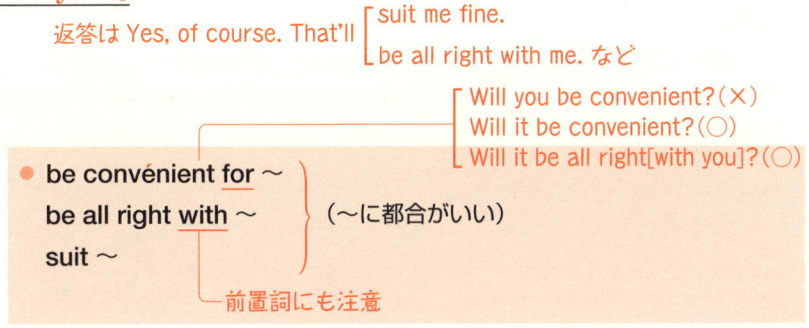

返答は Yes, of course. That'll { suit me fine. / be all right with me. など

- **be convénient for ～**
  be all right with ～　　（〜に都合がいい）
  suit ～
  ┗ 前置詞にも注意

  ┌ Will you be convenient?（×）
  │ Will it be convenient?（○）
  └ Will it be all right[with you]?（○）

147

■ 形容詞と会話 Great!(すごい！)のように形容詞1語だけでもよい

●「すばらしい」
great, fine, lovely, splendid,
capital(主要な，一流の), excellent(すぐれた),
supérb(すばらしい，上等な),
górgeous(豪華な，見事な),
magníficent(壮大な，とびきりすばらしい),
bréathtaking(はっと息をのむような) …

●「おもしろい」
interesting(興味をひく), amúsing(楽しませる),
excíting(興奮させるような), thrílling(ぞくぞくさせる),
boring(退屈な，つまらない), uninteresting(つまらない) …

●「まさか」
impóssible(ありえない), unbelíevable(信じられない),
incrédible(信じられない，すごい) …
Impossible! I can't believe it.(まさか，信じられないよ)

●「おいしい」
good, delicious, tasty, …

〔解答〕
A：What time shall I come and see you next week?
B：Friday afternoon will be most convenient for me. Would it be all right with you?

第 12 回

関係詞

TRACK 01

■ 関係詞節を含む文

文中の N ─先行詞という
　　　↑
　　S' + V' + X' + X'

日本語：表紙の破れた辞書
英　語：辞書　表紙の破れた

(1) ⬜S⬜ + V + C
　　　↑
　　(S') + V' + C'

　　　　　　　1つの文の中に
　　　　　　　SVXX と S'V'X'X'

(3) S + V + ⬜O⬜
　　　　　　↑
　　　　(prep. O') + S' + V'
　　　　～～～～～～
　　　　　"前置詞＋関係代名詞"
　　　　　という形で文をつなげる

(4) S + V + O, (S') + V' + O' + X'　　[..., who ...
　　　　　　→　　　　　　　　　　　　..., which ...
　　　　　　　　　　　　　　　　　→（前から後ろへ意味をとる）

1 英文(1)〜(12)の空所に入れるのに最も適当なものを，次の語句から選んで記入しなさい。

格変化がある　　　　先行詞を含む関係代名詞　　　関係副詞

who, whose, whom, which, / what, as, / when, where, why, / whoever, / of which, of which, for which, for whom, for what
　　　　　　└─anyone who ...　　　　　前置詞＋関係代名詞

150

(1) The man [(whose) suit is blue] is Mr. White's secretary.
　　　　　　スーツが青い人（青いスーツを着た人）　　　　秘書

> ■ もとの文を頭に浮かべる
>
> 　whose suit is blue ← His suit is blue.
> 　　所有格の関係代名詞　　　所有格の代名詞
> 　（who — whose — whom）　（he — his — him）

(2) The dictionary [the cover (of which) is torn] is mine.
　　辞書　　　　　　 whose cover is torn
　　　　　　　　　　　　　　　　　　　　　　（その）表紙が破れている

> ● the cover of which is torn ← The cover of the dictionary is torn.
> 　whose cover is torn ← its cover is torn
> 　先行詞が「人」でも「物」でも使われる

(3) The boy found the lost dog [(for which) its owner had been searching].
　　　　　　　　　 行方不明の犬　　　　　　　　　飼い主が探していた

> ● the lost dog for which its owner had been searching
> 　← Its owner had been searching for the lost dog.
> ● search（[家・部屋などを]捜す，捜索する）
> 　I searched my pockets for a coin.
> 　（ポケットをさぐってコインを捜した）
> ● search for（〜を捜し求める）　比較　{ search the room（部屋の中を捜す） / search for a room（部屋はないかと探す） }
> 　I searched for a missing key.
> 　（なくなったキーを探した）

(4) I met a boatman, / (who) kindly took me across the river (by ferry).
⇨ [非制限用法]
船頭に会うと，その船頭が…してくれた

- 非制限用法
  ..., who ... → and he kindly took me ...
- 制限用法
  I met a boatman who had taken me across the river by ferry.
  （私は，以前私をフェリーボートで川を渡らせてくれたことのある船頭に会った）

(5) There isn't enough money (for what) I want to buy.
買いたい物を買えるだけの金がない　　名詞節
私の買いたい物
(the thing which I want to buy)

- enough ... for ~（～するのに十分な…，～できるだけの…）
- what I want to buy ← the thing which I want to buy
  先行詞を含む関係代名詞　　what 1 語で表せる
  what I said（私が言ったこと）
  This is just what I wanted.
  （これは私がまさに欲しかった物だ→私がほしかったのはまさにこれだ）

(6) I believe / that swimming, [(which) is a good sport], makes people strong.
水泳（それはよいスポーツだが）体を丈夫にしてくれる

- ..., which ..., ... 文の途中に挿入し，補足的説明を加える

(7) You don't have to talk to [such people [(as) may ignore you]].

主格の関係代名詞
あなたを無視するかもしれないような人
those people who may ignore you.

- 関係代名詞 as
  such ~ as ... （…するような〜）　　先行詞に such がつくと関係代名詞は as となる
  as is often the case （よくあることだが）　―挿入的に使われる as ...
  She is late, as is often the case with her.
  （彼女にはよくあることだが，遅刻している）

(8) June and September are the months [(when) we have a lot of rain].
(= in which)

- 関係副詞 when
  the months <u>when</u> we have a lot of rain
  ← we have a lot of rain /then.　　then（副詞）の代わりに when ...（関係副詞）を使う
  in the months なら in which ...となる
  （前置詞＋関係代名詞）でつなぐ

(9) It is said / that Chicago is the city [(where) you can easily get lost].
(= in which)

> - 関係副詞 where
>   the city where you can easily get lost
>   ← you can easily get lost { there. } there(副詞)の代わりに where ...(関係副詞)を使う
>   { in the city なら in which ... となる }

(10) They will sell the car to [(**whoever**) arrives first].
　　　　　　　　　　　　　　　(= anyone who ...)

> - **whoever arrives first** ← **anyone who** arrives first.
>   　　　　　　　　　　　（最初に来た人は誰にでも）
> - **whatever he says** ← **anything that** he says
>   She objects to whatever he says.（彼の言うことなら何でも反対する）

(11) Bertrand Russell is one of the philósophers [(**for whom**) I have the greatest respect].
　　　　　　　　　　　　　　　　　　　　哲学者
「私が最大の敬意を抱く哲学者たちの１人だ」
　Bertrand Russell is one of the philosophers.
　I have the greatest respect for them.　　}を連結した文

(12) Margaret is no longer (**what**) she was (twenty years ago).
　　　　　　　　もはや…でない　　　　「20年前の彼女（の状態）」ということ
「Margaret はもはや 20 年前とは変わってしまっている」の意
　Margaret is no longer the girl (that) she was twenty years ago.

> - what she was twenty years ago
>   ← the girl (that) she was twenty years ago.

> 同様に　I'm no longer what I was yesterday.
> 　　　　I'm no longer the man (that) I was yesterday.

〔解答〕
(1) **whose**　　(2) **of which**　(3) **for which**　(4) **who**　　(5) **for what**
(6) **which**　 (7) **as**　　　 (8) **when**　　　(9) **where**　(10) **whoever**
(11) **for whom**　(12) **what**

2 それぞれの下線部に注意して，次の英文を日本語に訳しなさい。

(1) We went to <u>the door</u> of the old church, / <u>which</u> I was surprised to find open.

findの目的語(O´)にあたる！
先行詞は the door

× 「…行って，ドアを開けてみて驚いた」
○ I was surprised to find it open. （ドアが開いているのがわかって…）
　　　　　　　　　　　V´ O´ C´

◎「…行ってみたら，ドアが開いているのがわかって驚いた」

■ 関係代名詞節の考え方
① 先行詞は何か確かめる　………the door (of the old church)
② 関係詞の節中での働き(S´, O´など)………ここでは to find の O´
　を考える／
　元の文(S´+ V´+ O´+ X´)に戻してみる

2文に分けてみる◎

ここでは We went ... the old church.
I was surprised to <u>find</u> <u>it</u> <u>open</u>.
　　　　　　　　　　V´ O´ C´

(2) The burglar(強盗) tried to force the front door open, / which was found impossible.
    　　　　　　　　　　　 V 　　　　 O 　　　　C

玄関ドアを無理やり開けようとしたが，それは不可能だとわかった
それ＝前の文の内容(to force the front door open)をさす

- ..., which was found impossible ← but it was found impossible.
  　　　　　　　　　　　　　　　　　　　　（前の文の内容をさす）

■ 先行詞は何か
前文の内容をうける which
My dog was waiting for my arrival, which greatly surprised me. など

(3) There was something (in his face) [that curiously attracted most people].
    　　　　　　　　　（先行詞）
  × 「たいていの人たちを妙に引きつける彼の顔には何かがあった」
  ○ 「彼の顔にはたいていの人たちを妙に引きつけるところがあった」
  　　　　　　　　　　　　　　　　　　　　　　　（何か）

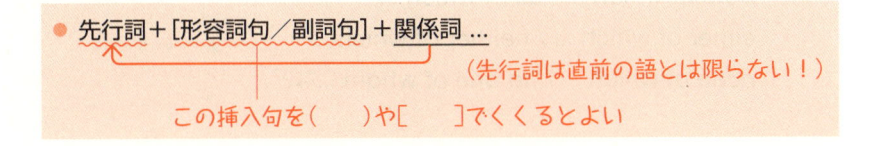

- 先行詞＋[形容詞句／副詞句]＋関係詞 ...
  　　　　　　　　　　　　　　　（先行詞は直前の語とは限らない！）
  この挿入句を（　）や[　]でくくるとよい

(4) (For most children) those parts (of the brain) [which control lánguage] are fully devéloped (by the age of nine).
　　　　　　　　　　　　　十分発達している　　　　　9歳までに

△言語をコントロールする脳の部分
○脳のうち言語能力を支配する部分

those がつく名詞は先行詞になりやすい

- **those** 〜 **which** ...（…の〜）　　those students in my class who ...
- **those** 〜 **who** ...（…の人たち）　（私のクラスの…のような学生）
- 先行詞＋[形容詞句／副詞句]＋関係詞 ...

ここでは of the brain を(　)でくくる

　　　　　　　〜から成り立つ　　小さな出来事の連続(→一連の小さな出来事)
(5) Human life consists of a succéssion of small events, /

each of which seems comparatively unimportant.
　　　　　　　　　　　　比較的つまらない
(and each of the events seems ...)

「人間生活は一連の小さな出来事から成り立ち，それらの出来事のひとつひとつは比較的重要ではないように思える」

- **each of which** ...
  both of which ... / **all of which** ...　　これらの形に
  either of which ... / **neither of which** ...　慣れておくこと
  none of which ... / **no one of whom** ...など

(6) Excitement is like a drug, / of which more and more will come to be required.

- of which more and more ... / more and more of which ...
  (← more and more of the drug will come ......)

〔解答〕
(1) 私たちが古い教会のドアのところへ行ってみると，そのドアが開いていたので私はびっくりした。
(2) どろぼうは正面のドアを無理に開けようとしたが，それは不可能だとわかった。
(3) 彼の顔には，どこかしら妙にたいていの人をひきつけるところがあった。
(4) たいていの子供たちにとって，脳の中の言語をつかさどる部分は9歳までにはすっかり発達している。
(5) 人間の生活は小さな出来事の連続から成り立っていて，ひとつひとつの出来事は比較的重要ではないように思える。
(6) 興奮は麻薬のようなもので，しだいに多くの量が要求されるようになってくるものだ。

TRACK 04

3 次の日本文を英語に直しなさい。

(1) ここが [(あなたの言っていた) スミスというアメリカ人が住んでいる] 家です。
　　　　　　　　　　　　　　　　Mr. Smith, an American　　　lives[is living]

　　× Here is the house ...
　　○ This is the house
　　　┌ in which ┐
　　　│ where   │ Mr. Smith, an American lives
　　　│ which   ┐
　　　└ (that) ┘ Mr. Smith, an American lives in.
　　　　　　　　　┌ you spoke of
　　　　　　　　　│ that you spoke of
　　　　　　　　　│ whom you spoke of
　　　　　　　　　└ of whom you spoke

> ● 次の短文を思い浮かべれば正確にできる
> This is the house.
> 　← He lives in the house.　──── in which でつなぐ
> 　　He lives there.　────────── where でつなぐ
> Mr. Smith, an American
> 　← You spoke of him.　────── of whom / whom ... of / that ... of / (that) ... of などでつなぐ

〔解答〕
This is the house (that) Mr. Smith, an American (that) you spoke of, lives in.

第12回 関係詞

TRACK 05

(2) (何週間もの間ぼくが恐れていた)日がついにやって来た。姉たちはぼくを取り囲み，「今日は(学校が始まる)日だよ」と言って，ぼくをつまみ上げた。

- at last / finally
- surround
- ○ picked me up
- × picked up me
- saying ...
- as they were saying ... （…と言いながら）

The day ⎡ finally came   [(which / that) I had dreaded]
        ⎣ came at last   for (many) weeks.
                                （when はダメ！）

My sisters surrounded me and picked me up,

⎡ saying, "This is the day ⎡ (when)   your school starts."
⎢   ⎢ (on which)
⎢   ⎣ (that)
⎢
⎣ saying (that) that was the day ⎡ (when)   my school ⎡ started.
                                 ⎢ (on which)   ⎣ was starting.
                                 ⎣ (that)

● 関係代名詞か関係副詞か

The day came at last.
 ← I had dreaded <u>the day</u>. (SVO) ─ 目的格の関係代名詞
                                         which / that を使う
                                         （関係副詞 when はダメ！）

This is the day.
 ← Your school starts <u>then</u>.
   Your school starts <u>on the day</u>. ─ ここに注目して
                                           when（関係副詞）
                                           または on which を使う

161

> 注意：次の覚え方は不十分
> the place where …（場所だから where）
> the time when …（時間だから when）   （△ / ✗）
> the reason why …（理由だから why）
>
> ⎛ the place (that / which) I visited （○）
> ⎜ the place where I visited （✗）
> ⎜ the place (that / which) I know well （○）   理解すること◎
> ⎝ the place where I know well （✗）

〔解答〕
The day came at last which I had dreaded for (many) weeks. My sisters surrounded me and picked me up, saying, "This is the day (when) your school starts."

第 13 回

比 較

TRACK 01

■ 比較構文

S + V + X + X の中のどこでも形容詞・副詞に比較の形が生じる

<u>as</u> / <u>so</u> Adj. / Adv. <u>as</u> S´ + V´ + X´ + X´
　　　　　　　　　　　　　　　　（省略が多い）

as ... as ～
so ... as ～ 〕（～と同じくらい…）の形

比較級 <u>than</u> S´ + V´ + X´ + X´
　　　　　　　　　　　（省略が多い）

It is cold.
→ It is <u>as</u> cold <u>as</u> (it was) yesterday. (昨日と同じくらい寒い)
→ It is colder <u>than</u> (it was) yesterday. (昨日より寒い)

1 次の文の（ ）内のうち最も適当なものを選び，○で囲みなさい。

　　　　　　　　　　　　　[3つ以上のうち]最も役立つ
(1) This machine is (the most useful, ⓘthe more useful, more useful) of the two.
　　　　　　　　　　　　　　　　　　[2つのうち]より役立つほう
　　2つのうち

> ● the 比較級 of the two（[2つのうち] ～なほう）
> 　the 最上級 of all（[3つ以上の] すべてのうち最も～）

164

> Which is the better of the two?
> — This one is (the better of the two).
> Which is the best of all?
> — This one is (the best of all).

(2) Tom has better memory than (any other boy, all other boys, all the boys) in his class. ほかのどの男の子より記憶力がよい

　　最上級とともに
　　Tom has the best memory of all the boys.

> ● 比較級 than any other ＋単数名詞（他のどの…より〜）　⎫
> 　no other — is 比較級 than 〜（〜より…な—はない）　⎬ [最上級]の意味
> → the 最上級 of all the 〜s（すべての〜のうち最も…）　⎭ を表す形式
>
> 　　　　　　⎧ the highest mountain in Japan.
> 　Mt. Fuji is ⎨
> 　　　　　　⎩ higher than any other mountain in Japan.
> 　No other mountain in Japan is higher than Mt. Fuji.

　　　　　　　否定文　　　　　　　　　　　　　　　　　　　[still]
(3) He was not able to keep himself, / (no less, much less, nevertheless) his family.　自分を養う　　（ましてや〜でない）
　　まして家族を養うことはできない

> ● ……, much[still] more 〜（…まして〜）
> 　It's hard to speak English, much more to write it.
> 　（話すのはむずかしい，まして書くのはなおさらだ）
> ● not ……, much[still] less 〜（…でない，まして〜でない）

> He can't even walk, much less run.
> (歩くことさえできない，まして走ることはなおさらできない)
> - **not ......, let alone ~**（~はもちろん…でない）

(4) Mr. Minton's is the third (large, larger, **largest**) house (in this town).
　　　　　　　　　　　　　　　　　3番目に大きな家
　　　　2番目に大きな家なら the second largest house

> - **the 最上級**（最も~，いちばん~）
> - **the second 最上級**（2番目に~）
>   Osaka is the second largest city in Japan.
>   **the third 最上級**（3番目に~）

　　　　　　　3歳だけ年下(younger than I[me])
(5) John is three years junior (than I, than me, **to me**), / but excels (than I, than me, **me**) (in knowledge and wisdom).
　　　　　私よりすぐれている　　　　　　　　　　知識と知恵の点で
　　　　　(he is superior to me)

> - 比較級を使わない比較表現　　　　　than ではなく to
>   **sénior to** ~（~より年上）
>   **júnior to** ~（~より年下）
>   **supérior to** ~（~よりすぐれている）
>   **inférior to** ~（~より劣っている）
>   A **excéls** B.（A は B よりすぐれている）
>   **prefér** A **to** B.（B より A を好む）——like A better than B
>   A is **préferable to** B.（A のほうが B より好ましい）
>   ↑　　　　　　　　　 └ than ではなく to
>   (more は不要)

〔解答〕
(1) This machine is <u>the more useful</u> of the two.
(2) Tom has better memory than <u>any other boy</u> in his class.
(3) He was not able to keep himself, <u>much less</u> his family.
(4) Mr. Minton's is the third <u>largest</u> house in this town.
(5) John is three years junior <u>to me</u>, but excels <u>me</u> in knowledge and wisdom.

TRACK 02

2 次の英文を（　）内の指示にしたがって書き換え，下の文を完成させなさい。

(1) The bird was <u>half the size of</u> an eagle. （large を用いて）
　　　　　　　　　　ワシの大きさの半分／ワシの半分の大きさだ

　The bird was <u>half as large as an eagle</u>.

This bird is large.（この文が基本形）
　→ <u>as</u> large <u>as</u> ～（～と同じ大きさだ）
　→ <u>half</u> <u>as</u> large <u>as</u> ～（～の半分の大きさだ）
　→ <u>twice</u> <u>as</u> large <u>as</u> ～（～の2倍の大きさだ）

● 倍数の表現
　half, twice
　three times　　｝ as ... as ～（～の一倍…）
　ten times
　これらを <u>as ... as ～の直前に置く</u>（語順に注意◎）
　　　just[exactly, precisely] as ... as ～（～とまさに同じだけ…）
　　　　　　　└── これらと同じ感じで

　　　　年をとるにつれて
(2) [<u>As</u> he grew <u>older</u>], he became <u>more</u> convínced of the folly of the public.
　　　　　　　　　　　　　　　ますます～を確信するようになった
　一般大衆の愚かさ，愚行

　　（The older ... で始まる文に）

第13回 比較

[The older he grew], the more convinced he became of the folly of the public.
　C'　　S'　V'　　　　　　　C　　　　S　　V

一種の倒置形だから，もとの文を思い浮かべれば間違えない

前半　he grew older → The older he grew
後半　he became more convinced of ...
　　　　→ the more convinced he became of ...

- **The 比較級 ..., the 比較級 ...**
  The older ..., the more ......
  （年をとればとるほどその分だけますます…）

(3) It is not so much his idéals as his ideas / that are bad.
　　　　　　　　　　　理想　　　　　考え
　　　　　　　　　　　　　　　　　　　　（悪いのは…だ）

（rather than を用いて）

ideals ＜ ideas（理想よりむしろ考えの方）

It is his ideas rather than his ideals that are bad.

- **not so much A as B**（B ほど A ではない→ A というよりむしろ B）
  → A ＜ B → B rather than A （A というよりむしろ B）
  不等号を思い浮かべれば間違えない

〔解答〕
(1) The bird was half as large as an eagle.
(2) The older he grew, the more convinced he became of the folly of the public.
(3) It is his ideas rather than his ideals that are bad.

3 それぞれの下線部に注意して，次の英文を日本語に訳しなさい。

TRACK 03

(1) George was a nice, kindly, intelligent fellow / and he seemed to take as great a fancy to me [as I took to him].

親切な，思いやりのある，聡明な男
take a fancy to ～（～を好む）
語順に注意！
「私が彼を好むのと同じくらい私を好いてくれているようだった」

● 語順に注意
　take a great fancy to ...（…を大いに好む）に as ... as ～ を用いると
　take as great a fancy to ... as ～ という語順になる

(2) There is nothing too little [for so little a créature as man]. It is by studying little things / that we attain the great art of having as little misery and as much happiness (as possible).

小さすぎるものはない
人間くらい小さな生き物（語順に注意）
of ～という技術を得る
なるべく小さな不幸となるべく多くの幸福（を得るという技術）
小さな物事を研究することによって（こそ…）（ここを強調する構文）
studyは「よく観察する，勉強する，じっくり研究する」の意

● a little creature
　→ as little a creature as man
　　 so little a creature as man 〕（人間くらい小さな生き物）
● as ... as possible
● as ... as one can 〕（できるだけ…）

170

第13回　比　較

> Come as early { as possible. / as you can.
> (できるだけ早く来なさい)

(3) These old pictures are all the more précious nowadays (because they are rare).
　　　　　　　　　　　　　　　　　　　貴重な、価値のある　今日では
希少であるだけにその分ますます貴重だ
貴重な + α
希少だからその分ますます〜

She loves him all the more [because he is childish].
彼を愛している + ○
子どもっぽいだけにその分だけますます〜

■ the 比較級 ... because ...
　(all) the 比較級 ... because ...（…であるだけにますます〜）

　(all) the 比較級 for 〜（〜であるだけにますます〜）

(4) [The happier a man is], the longer he lives on; [the more he suffers], the sooner he dies.
　　　　　　　　　　　　　　　　生き続ける

・幸福であればあるほど（その分だけ）ますます長生きする
・多く苦しめば苦しむほど（その分だけ）ますます早く死ぬ

- [the 比較級 ...,] the 比較級 ...
  　　　　　　　　（…であればあるほどその分だけますます…）

  [The more you practice,] the better you become at it.
  　　　　　　　　　　　　　　　C　S　　V
  （練習すればするほど[それだけますます]それがうまくなる）

(5) The largest fortune cannot satisfy human wishes, / but (with care and method) the smallest one can do it.
　　　　　財産　　　　～を満たす　　人間の願い,望み
　　　　　　　　　　　　　　　　　　　　　　　　　　fortune　　satisfy human wishe
　　注意と方法

（×）「最大の財産は人間の望みをかなえないが、…」

（○）「いくら財産があっても人間の望みをかなえられないが」

（×）「…最少の財産はそれができる」

（○）「いくら少ない財産でもそれができる」

■ 最上級の文脈による意味

The richest man in the world cannot buy everything.
　　　　　　　　　　　　　　　　┌─部分否定─┐
文脈によって even ～の意味を含む　　すべてを買えるわけではない,
　　　　　　　　　　　　　　　　　何から何まで買うわけにはいかない

even the richest man ...

（世の中でいちばん金持ちの人でも）

The wisest man sometimes makes mistakes.

（最も賢い人でもときには間違えるものだ）

〔解答〕
(1) ジョージは親切で思いやりのある聡明な男で，私が彼を好きなのと同じくらい彼も私を好いてくれているように思えた。
(2) 人間のような小さな生き物にとっては，小さすぎる物など何もない。私たちが苦痛をなるべく少なく幸福をなるべく多くするというすばらしい技術を達成するのは，小さな物事を研究することによってである。
(3) これらの古い絵画は，それらが希少であるだけに今日ではいっそう貴重である。
(4) 人間は幸福な生活を送れば，それだけ長生きする。苦しみが多ければ，それだけ早死にする。
(5) いくら大きな財産でも人間の望みをことごとくかなえるわけにはいかないが，周到な注意と方法をもってすれば，最少の財産でもそれができる。

TRACK 05

4 次の日本文を英語に直しなさい。ただし，(1)～(4)は（ ）内の指示に従うこと。

(1) トムは私の<u>10</u>倍くらい切手を持っています。
（<u>as, as, has, have, I, postage stamps, Tom, about ten times</u> に1語を加えて，正しく配列せよ）

Tom has <u>many</u> postage stamps.　この文が基本（much は×）

→ Tom has as many postage stamps as I have.（私と同じくらい…）

→ Tom has <u>about ten times</u> as <u>many</u> postage stamps as I have.
　　　　　　この位置に　　　　　　　　　　　　　（私の10倍くらい）

as ... as の直前に twice, ten times, ... など

● **about ten times as ... as ...**
　← **Tom has many postage stamps.**
　この基本文ができていないと語順を誤りやすい◎

参考
「トムは私の何倍くらい切手を持っていると思う？」
（こういう発想は英語にはない）
How many times <u>as</u> many postage stamps <u>as</u> I have <u>do you think</u> Tom has?
となるべきところ　　　　　　　　　　　　└ p.285 を参照

第13回　比　較

(2) けさはいつもより1時間早く目が覚めた。

(hour, I, than, up, an, usual, woke, this morning に1語を加えて，正しく配列せよ)

I woke up early this morning.　この文が基本

→ I woke up earlier than usual this morning.
　　　　　　　↑
　　an hour (1時間だけ早く)

- 比較級 ... than usual（いつもより…）
  ← I woke up early this morning.
    early — earlier — earliest

knowledge
(3) [知識があればあるほど] 成功する見込みは大きい。

(likely, the more, the more, you are, you have, to succeed に1語を加えて，正しく配列せよ)

前半　You have much knowledge. → The more knowledge you have,

後半　you are likely to succeed. → the more likely you are to succeed.

　　　　　　　　　　　　　　この語順が大事！

- be likely to 〜（〜しそうだ）

175

(4) 私はこんなに恐ろしい交通事故を見たことがありません。
((a) 比較級を含む文に，(b) 最上級を含む文に)

(a) <u>I have never seen a more terrible traffic accident (than this)</u>.
(b) <u>This is the most terrible traffic accident / that I have ever seen</u>.
(これまで見たうちでいちばん～)

最上級を強める表現

> ● **never ... 比較級 than ～** 最上級の意味を表す
> **the 最上級 ～ that ... ever ...**
>   これまでに…した(うちで)最も～な
> **never ... as ... as ～** ┐ I've never seen so[as] terrible a traffic
> **never ... so ... as ～** ┘ accident (as this). 語順に注意
> **never ... such a ... as ～** I've never seen such a terrible accident (as this).

176

第 13 回　比　較

(5) 外国人はよく日本語は習得するのがたいへん難しいと言います。しかし，英語が日本語よりもやさしいとは私には思われません。

　　foreigners / people from abroad　　very hard to master

Foreigners often say (that)

Japanese [is very hard to master, / is very difficult to learn,] but ...

I don't think ...
I can hardly believe ...
it doesn't seem to me that ...

● **hard to ～**（～しにくい，～するのが難しい）

　　It is hard to read this book.
　　This book is hard to read.

　Japanese is hard to master.
　Japanese is difficult to learn.

　　形容詞を修飾する不定詞

● **A is easier than B.**（A は B よりやさしい）
　easy － easier － easiest

〔解答〕
(1) Tom has about ten times as <u>many</u> postage stamps as I have.
(2) I woke up an hour <u>earlier</u> than usual this morning.
(3) The more <u>knowledge</u> you have, the more likely you are to succeed.
(4) (a) I have never seen a <u>more terrible</u> traffic accident (than this).
　 (b) This is <u>the most terrible</u> traffic accident that I have ever seen.
(5) Foreigners often say (that) Japanese is very difficult to master, but I can hardly believe that English is easier (to learn) than Japanese.

第14回

否定・比較

TRACK 01

誤りやすい
Man thinks of nothing less than of death.
何を考えないといって死ほど(少ししか)考えないものはない。
(死について最も考えない)

■ 「否定＋比較」の考え方—次の2通り

(例) We expected nothing less than an attack. 攻撃
① 私たちは少なくとも攻撃くらいはあると思った(≧攻撃)
②《まれ》よもや攻撃があるとは思わなかった(⇒最上級の意)
We least expected an attack.(いちばん少ししか…)

1 次の(a), (b)の2文がほぼ同じ意味になるように，空所に適当な語を入れなさい。

(1) (a) It is the most important thing / to have self-confidence. 自信を持つ
   (b) (Nothing) is so important / (as) to have confidence in yourself.
   自分自身を信頼する

● 否定語 ＋ as / so ... as ～（～ほど…なものはない）（⇒最上級）
No other mountain in Japan is <u>as</u> high <u>as</u> Mt. Fuji.
[so]

第14回 否定・比較

(2) (a) (To almost all creatures) their homes are the dearest places in the world.
   （生き物）   （最も重要な）

 (b) (To almost all creatures), (no) other places in the world are (dearer) than their homes.

> 否定語 + 比較級 than ～ （～以上…なものはない）（⇒最上級）
> No other mountain in Japan is higher than Mt. Fuji.

(3) (a) A bat is no more a bird than a rat is.
   （こうもり）   （ねずみ）

 (b) A bat is not a bird, (any) (more) than a rat is.
   少しも more ではない（強い否定）   (not any = no)
   →等号を頭に浮かべるとよい!!

   「こうもりが鳥である程度は，
   ねずみが鳥である程度と同じだ」
   →「こうもりはねずみが鳥でないのと
   　同様に鳥ではない」

> no more … than ～ （ちっとも～以上ではない，同じかそれ以下だ
>   ⇨～でないのと同様…ではない）
> not … any more than ～
>   └(= no)

A bat is a bird. ≒ A rat is a bird.
程度が同程度
（またそれ以下）   否定的な例
         The baby is no bigger than a doll.
         赤ちゃん ≒ 人形
                  └大きくないもの
                   の例（×ゴジラ）

(4) (a) Only ten persons were present at the meeting.
(b) There were (no) (more) than ten persons present at the meeting.

多くはない感じ / 少ない感じ
→たったの10人しか出席していなかった

no less than a thousand people
└ 多い感じ
→1000人もの人たち
(as many as 1000 people)

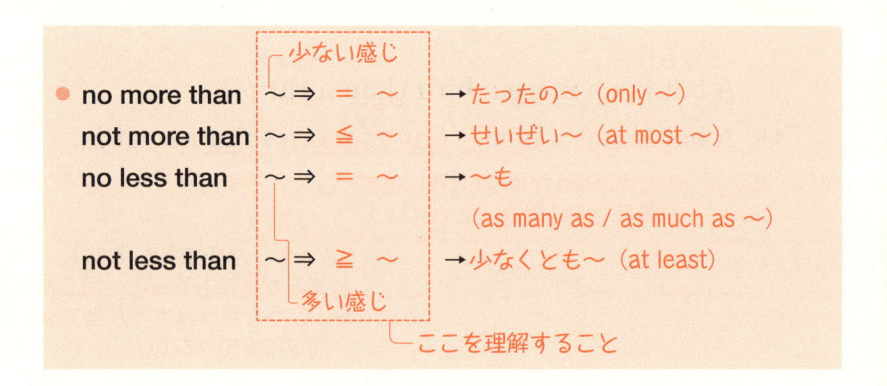

- **no more than** 〜 ⇒ = 〜 →たったの〜 (only 〜) ┐少ない感じ
- **not more than** 〜 ⇒ ≦ 〜 →せいぜい〜 (at most 〜)
- **no less than** 〜 ⇒ = 〜 →〜も
  (as many as / as much as 〜)
- **not less than** 〜 ⇒ ≧ 〜 →少なくとも〜 (at least) ┘多い感じ

ここを理解すること

〔解答〕
(1) **Nothing** is so important **as** to have confidence in yourself.
(2) **To almost all creatures, no** other places in the world are **dearer** than their homes.
(3) **A bat is not a bird, any more** than a rat is.
(4) **There were no more** than ten persons at the meeting.

第14回　否定・比較

TRACK 02

2 それぞれの下線部に注意して，各組の文の意味を比較しなさい。

(1) (a) I lay down <u>not so much</u> to sleep <u>as</u> to think.
　　　　　　　　　　　　　　　　　　　　ここが急所
　　　　　　　　　　　　　　　　(⇨ to sleep ＜ to think)

(b) He did <u>not so much as</u> say 'Thank you.'
　　　　　　　　　　　　　　(→ not even) どうして？
　　　　　　　　so much as ～は「～程度」の意

(c) She walked past me [<u>without so much as</u> nodding]. 会釈する
　　　　　　　　　　　　　　(→ without even ～) どうして？

(a) 眠ろうと思うよりむしろ考えようと思って横になった。

(b) 彼は「ありがとう」┌と言うくらいのこともしなかった。
　　　　　　　　　　└とも言わなかった。

(c) 彼女は会釈┌するくらいのこともせずに
　　　　　　　└すらしないで

　　　　　　　　　　　　　　　　私のそばを通り過ぎた。
　　　　　so much as ～は「～と同程度のこと」

- **not so much A as B** ⇒ A ＜ B
  → B rather than A （A というよりむしろ B）
- **not so much as ～** ⇐ not ＋ so much as ～
  　　　　　　　　　（～程度のこともしない，～すらしない）

  without so much as ～ ⇐ without ＋ so much as ～
  　　　　　　　　　　　　（～程度のこともせずに，～すらせずに）

〔解答〕
(a) 私は眠るというより考えようと思って横になった。
(b) 彼は「ありがとう」と言うくらいのこともしなかった。
→彼は「ありがとう」も言わなかった。
(c) 彼女は会釈をするといった程度のこともせずに私の横を通り過ぎた。
→彼女は会釈もせずに私の横を通り過ぎた。

(2) (a) Helen is <u>never more</u> attractive <u>than</u> when she is working. （⇨最上級の意味）

　　　　　most attractive when she is working

(b) Helen is <u>no more</u> attractive <u>than</u> <u>her mother is</u>. ←あまり魅力的でない例
　　　　　　　　　　　　　　　　　　　　　　　（Helen ＝母）

(c) Helen is <u>not more</u> attractive <u>than</u> <u>her sister Jane</u>.
　　　　　　　　　　　　　　　　　　　　　　　（Helen ≦ Jane）

(d) Helen is <u>no less</u> attractive <u>than</u> the movie star.
　　　　　　　　　　　　　　　　　　　　　　　（Helen ＝映画スター）

(e) Helen is <u>not less</u> attractive <u>than</u> the movie star.
　　　　　　　　　　　　　　　　　　　　　　　（Helen ≧映画スター）

(a) ヘレンは　働いているときほど魅力的なときはない。
　　　　　　　働いているときが最も魅力的だ。

(b) （Helen ＝母）ヘレンは母親と同じくらいしか魅力的ではない。

(c) （Helen ≦ Jane）ヘレンは姉［妹］のジェーンほど魅力的ではない。
　　　　　　　　　　　　　　　（魅力ではせいぜいジェーン程度だ）

(d) (Helen＝スター)ヘレンは映画スターに劣らず魅力的だ。

(魅力ではちっとも劣らない)

(e) (Helen≧スター)ヘレンは映画スターにまさるとも劣らず魅力的だ。

- never 比較級 than 〜（〜以上に…なものはない）（⇒ 最上級）
- A is no more ... than B. → A ＝ B（少しも B 以上でない）
  　　強い否定　　　　much ではない感じ
  　[It's not easy.（容易でない）
  　[It's no easy job.（生やさしくないよ）
  A is not more ... than B. → A ≦ B（せいぜい B 程度）
  A is no less ... than B. → A ＝ B（B に劣らず…だ）
  A is not less ... than B. → A ≧ B（B にまさるとも劣らず…だ）
  　　　　　　　　　　little ではない感じ

〔解答〕
(a) ヘレンは働いているときほど魅力的なときはない。
　　→ヘレンは働いているときが最も魅力的だ。
(b) ヘレンは母親と同じくらいしか魅力的ではない。
　　→母親は魅力的ではないが，ヘレンも同じように魅力的ではない。
(c) ヘレンは姉(妹)のジェーンほど魅力的ではない。
(d) ヘレンは映画スターに劣らず(同じように)魅力的だ。
(e) ヘレンは映画スターにまさるとも劣らず魅力的だ。

(3) (a) It is <u>nothing more than</u> an accident. (＝事故)

　　　　　　　　　　　　　　　　　much でない感じ。大したことはないというニュアンス

(b) It is <u>nothing less than</u> an invasion. (＝侵略)

　　　　　　　　　　　　　　little ではない感じ
　　　　　　　　　　　　　　大変なこと

(a) <u>単なる事故にすぎない。</u>

(b) <u>まさに侵略にほかならない。</u>

● A is nothing <u>more</u> than B. → A ＝ Ⓑ　much ではない感じ
　A is nothing <u>less</u> than B. → A ＝ Ⓑ　little ではない感じ

〔解答〕
(a) それは偶然以上の何物でもない。→ それは偶然にすぎない。
(b) それは侵略以下の何物でもない。→ それはまさに侵略行為だ。

第14回　否定・比較

3 それぞれの下線部に注意して，次の英文を日本語に訳しなさい。

(1) Nothing will cause another to lose confidence in you more readily than a broken promise.
  - S: Nothing
  - V: will cause
  - O: another
  - C: to lose confidence in you
  - 人にあなたの信頼を失わせる
  - more readily: たやすく
  - a broken promise: 破られた約束→約束を破ること

(→ A broken promise will cause another to lose confidence in you most readily.)

- **Nothing ... 比較級 than ～.**（～ほど…なものはない）(→ 最上級)
- **cause ... to ～**（…が～する原因となる，…に～させる）
  (例) Smog causes plants to die.（スモッグのために植物が枯れてしまう）
    - S: Smog　V: causes　O: plants　C: to die
    - （植物が枯れる）

〔解答〕 約束を破ることほど容易に，あなたに対する信用を人に失わせるものはないだろう。

(2) I have often imagined / what my feelings would be [if a doctor told me / that I had a fatal disease and had no more than a little time to live].
  - I have often imagined: よく想像してみた
  - what my feelings would be: 私の気持ちはどんなだろうか
  - no more（= only ～）
  - told me: 仮定法過去（もし医師が言ったら）
  - a fatal disease: 致命的な病気
  - no more than a little time to live: 余命いくばくもない（ほんの少ししか生きる時間がない）

> much でない感じ
> ↓
> ● no more than 〜 → only 〜
> 　　　　　　　　（たった〜しか）

〔解答〕　もし医師から致命的な病気にかかっていて余命がわずかしかないと告げられたら，私はどう感じるだろうかと何度も想像してみたことがある。

　　　　　　創り出す，生み出す　　　観察力
(3) We cannot create an observing faculty any more / than we can create a memory.
　　　　記憶力を創り出す　　　　　　　　　　　　　　　否定的な感じ

観察力を生み出す ＝ 記憶力を生み出す
　　　　　程度が同じ

「観察力を生み出すのは記憶力を生み出せる程度と同じくらいできない」という言い方

> ● not ... any more than 〜　（…は〜と同じように…でない）
> ● no more ... than 〜　（〜でないのと同様に…ではない／…でないのは〜でないのと同じだ）

〔解答〕　私たちは記憶力を創り出すことができないのと同様に，観察能力を創り出すことはできない。
　　→私たちは観察能力を創り出すことはできないが，それは記憶力を創り出すことができないのと同じである。

第14回　否定・比較

(4) I know no more disagreeable trouble [into which an author may plunge himself] [than of a quarrel with his critics].

> ● no 比較級 … than ～（～以上に…はない）(→ 最上級)
> ここでは「批評家との口論以上に不愉快な[ほどいやな]ごたごたを私は知らない」
> (→「私が知るごたごたで批評家との言い争いがいちばんいやなごたごただ」の意)

〔解答〕　著者が陥るごたごたで，批評家との論争（のごたごた）ほどいやなものを私は知らない。

TRACK 04

4 次の日本文を英語に訳しなさい。

was not so hard as I had expected
[as]　　　（過去完了）

その問題は思っていたほど難しくなかったので，/（ほんの 10 分くらいで）解くことができた。

answer the question（[試験]問題に答える）
solve the problem（[厄介な]問題を解決する）

The question was ...
The questions were ...
で書き出す（[解答]を参照）

in only ten minutes
in no more than ten minutes

（10 分以上はかからずに，ほんの 10 分で）

- **not as ... as ~**
  not so ... as ~ 　（～ほど…でない）
  not 比較級 than ~（～以上に…でない）
- **no more than ~**（たったの～，わずか～）(only ~)

〔解答〕

　The question was not so hard as I had expected, / so I was able to answer it in no more than ten minutes.

　The questions were less difficult than I had expected, / so it did not take me more than ten minutes to answer them.
　　　　　　　　　easier

第15回

否 定

■ 慣用的な否定表現

― 部分否定，二重否定などがある
― 否定語(not, never)などを含まない否定表現に注意

1 次の文が( )内の文とほぼ同じ意味になるように，空所に適当な1語を入れなさい。

(1) The windows are (too) dirty (to see through).
　(= The windows are so dirty / that we cannot see through them.)
　　　　　　　　　　　汚れているので先が見通せない
　　ここにも注意

> ● too ... to ～（～するには…すぎる，…なので～できない）
> ⇄ so ... that ... cannot ～

― but = except(～以外の)
「安全以外なら何でも」
→「安全とだけは言ってくれる」
→決して安全ではない

(2) That little bridge is (anything) but safe.
　(= That little bridge is not at all safe.)
　　　　　　　　　　「まったく～でない」（強い否定）

> ● anything but ～ / not at all ～ （決して～ではない）
> 強い否定を表す　She is anything but beautiful.
> 　　　　　　　(kind, honest... 何でもいいが beautiful だけはダメ!?)

― 省略可

(3) Mother is (far) from (being) pleased; she is very angry.
　(= Mother is not at all pleased; she is very angry.)
　　　　　　　　満足しているどころか，とても怒っている

第 15 回　否　定

- **far from ～**（～からほど遠い → とても～ではない）
- **free from ～**（～から解放されている → ～がない）
    - 名詞 care, fear, prejudice など
    （心配，不安，偏見などがない）

(4) Few people are (free) from cares.　　名詞
　　　　　　　　　　　　　　　　　　　　It's far from dangerous.
　　(= Few people are without cares.)　　It's free from danger.
　　　　　　　　　　　　　　　　　　　　　　　　　　　（危険がない）
　　　「心配事のない人はほとんどいない」
　　否定語
　　（ほとんど～でない）（a few は肯定的）

　　　　　　　　　分別がある
(5) He knows (better) than to tell a lie.「うそをつくほどばかじゃない」
　　　　　　　　　　　　　　　　　　　　「分別があるからうそはつかない」
　　(= He is above telling a lie.)
　　　　～を超越している，～のレベルの人ではない

　　　He is the last man to tell a lie.（彼はうそをつくような人ではない）

- **know better**（分別がある，ばかではない）
- **know better than to ～**
    - I know better than to trust him.
    - 彼を信用するほどばかじゃない
    - ばかじゃないから信用しない
- **be above ～ing**（[～を超越して] ～しない）
    - 「～を超えている」
    - It's above me.（私の理解を超えている，私にはとうてい理解できない）

(6) The car (failed) to climb the hill.
(= The car was unable to climb the hill.)
　　　　　　～できなかった

- **fail to ～**（～しない，できない）
  - fail in ～（～に失敗する）
  - fail to ～ → 否定に近い

  He often fails to keep his words.（よく約束を守らない）
- **be unable to ～**（～できない）
- **never fail to ～ / don't fail to ～ / be sure to ～**（必ず～する）

  肯定になる

  Never fail
  Don't fail } to write to me.
  Be sure 　（必ず手紙をちょうだいね）

TRACK 02

(7) His ideas are sometimes [beyond my comprehension. (more) than I can understand.
(= I sometimes cannot understand his ideas.)
　　　　　　　　　　　　　彼の考えが理解できないことがある

- **more than ... can ～**（～できる以上 → ～できない）

  He has more money than is needed.
  （必要以上のお金を…）
  →必要でないくらい金を…

- **beyond ～**（～を超えている，とうてい～でない）

  beyond description（描写できない）

(8) (What) is the use of arguing with a child?
　　(= It is no use / arguing with a child.)
　　　　　　　　　　　「子供と言い争ってもむだだ」

> ● **What is the use of ～ing ...?**（～して何の役に立つのか？）
> 　　　　　　　　　　　　　　　　→何の役にも立たない）
>
> **It is no use ～ing ...**
> **There's no use (in) ～ing ....**　　（～しても何の役にも立たない）

(9) (Who) knows when the toothache will come?
　　(= Nobody knows when the tóothache will come.)
　　　　　　　　　　　　歯痛がいつ起きるか
　　　　だれにわかるだろうか → だれにもわからない〈反語〉

> ● **Who ...?**
> 　　Who could wish for more?
> 　　（これ以上だれが望めようか）（→ Nobody could ...）
> 　　（申し分ない）
> 　　There's nothing more to be desired.
> 　　Who'll believe that?（→ Nobody will ...）
> ● **How ...?**
> 　　How can I do that?
> 　　→ I can never do that.
> 　　I can't do that in any way.（どうしてもできない）

(10) Tom was the (last) man [that I expected to see in such a place.]
　　　会うなんて思ってもみなかった
　　(= I never expected to see Tom in such a place.)

> ● the last ... that ... / the last ... to ～
>   (～する最後の… → とうてい～しない)
>   He's the last boy ⎡that would be loved ⎤by girls.(!)
>   　　　　　　　　 ⎣to be loved　　　　　 ⎦

(11) I can never thank you (enough).
　　　　　　　　　　　　　　　　　［× 十分感謝できない　　　　［十分ではな
　　　　　　　　　　　　　　　　　 ○ いくら感謝しても　　　　　 いくらい
　　(= I don't know how to thank you.)
　　　　お礼の申しようもない(→大変感謝している)

> ● can never ～ enough　 ⎫ どんなに～してもいいくらいだ
>   cannot ... too ～　　 ⎬ You can't be too careful in choosing your friends.

　　　どうしても～できない　　　　　独創的なことを思いつく
(12) I cannot, for the (life) of me, think of anything original.
　　(= It is quite impossible / for me to think of anything original.)
　　　　　まったく不可能

> ● 否定語を強める語句
>   cannot ～ for the life of me
>   　　　　　　　　(絶対に／死んでも→どうしても～できない)
>   can never ～ / cannot ～ at all (決して～できない)
>   (not ... ever)

第15回 否定

- not ... at all / not ... whatever（まったく〜でない）
  └─否定語を強める

  She shows no interest in politics whatever.
  （政治にはまったく興味がない）

  not ... in the least（少しも〜でない）
- by no means（[どんな手段を使っても]決して〜でない）

  in no way（[どんな点からも]決して〜でない）

  in no sense（[いかなる意味でも]決して…でない）

〔解答〕
(1) too (2) anything (3) far (4) free (5) better (6) failed
(7) more (8) What (9) Who (10) last (11) enough (12) life

TRACK 03

2 否定語に注意して，次の英文を日本語に訳しなさい。

(1) I haven't read both his novels, / but (judging from the
　　　　　　　　　　　　　　　　　　　　〜から判断すると

one I have read), he seems to be a prómising writer.
　novel　　　　　　　　　　　　　　　　　将来有望な作家

　×「私は彼の小説を両方とも読んでいない」
　○「私は彼の小説を両方とも読んだわけではない」（片方は読んだ[かもしれない]）

> ■ **部分否定と全部否定**
> ● not ... both（両方とも〜したわけではない）
> 　not ... either / neither（両方とも〜でない）
> ● not ... every 〜 / not ... all 〜（すべて〜なわけではない）
> 　not ... any 〜（どれも〜でない）

〔解答〕 私は彼の小説を2冊とも読んだわけではないが，私が読んだほう（の小説）から判断すると，彼はかなり有望な作家であるように思える。

第15回 否定

(2) Mother was sure / that her four boys were the best little boys in New York. Other people didn't always agree with her, / but she didn't know it.

きっと…だと思っていた (sure)
必ずしも〜ではない (didn't always)
→ always disagreed なら「いつも一致しなかった」
〜に同意する、考えが一致する (agree with)

- **not always**（いつも〜するとは限らない）
  always ... not（いつも…しない）
- **not nécessarily**（必ずしも…ではない）
- **not exáctly**（まさに…というわけではない）

〔解答〕 母は自分の4人の男の子たちはニューヨークで最も良い子たちだと思っていた。他人は必ずしも母と考えが合うわけではなかったのだが、母はそれに気づかなかった。

(3) We cannot read a good and interesting book for an hour without being the better for it.

本を読んだ分だけますます（the 比較級 for 〜）
良くなる 向上する

それだけ向上せずには…を読めない〈二重否定〉
→…を読めば必ずそれだけ向上する（○）

■ 二重否定など
- **cannot ... without 〜ing**
  never ... without 〜ing 〕（…すれば必ず〜する）

〔解答〕 すぐれたおもしろい本を1時間も読めば、必ずそのために向上するものだ。

(4) 賞賛を超えている→賞賛しきれないほど立派

[Because a man is beyond praise], it does not follow that
〜だからといって…ということにはならない

his every idea is too good to be looked into.
その人のことごとく　　調べてみるにはあまりにも良すぎる
の考えが　　　　　　→とても立派で吟味される必要がない

> It follows that ...([したがって]…ということになる)の否定形
>   ↓
> ● Because ..., it does not follow that ...
>   　（…だからといって…ということにはならない）
> ● beyond 〜（〜を超えている，〜よりすぐれている）
> ● too ... to 〜（〜するには…すぎる，…なので〜できない）

〔解答〕　ある人がとてもほめつくせないほど立派だからといって，その人の考えがことごとく立派で吟味の余地がないことにはならない。

(5) 　　　　　　　　　　詩人　　芸術家　　　哲学者
There is hardly a poet, artist, philósopher, or a man

of science, / whose genius was not oppósed by parents,
　科学者　　　　　　　　　　　　　　反対される
guardians, or teachers.
　保護者　　　　　　　才能，天分

反対されなかった…はほとんどいなかった〈二重否定〉
→ほとんどの…は反対された，という肯定の意味になる

> ● hardly ... not 〜（〜でない…はほとんどいない，ほとんどは〜だ）

第15回　否定

〔解答〕　詩人，芸術家，哲学者，または科学者で，その天分が両親，保護者，教師たちの反対を受けなかった者はほとんどない。

(6) It is not necessary / to do well in everything. There are
　　　　　　　　　　　　　　　すべてにうまくいく必要はない〈部分否定〉

práctically no people (who can do that), except, maybe, a
事実上，実際　　　　　　　　　　　　　　～を除いて，～以外は　　　多分，おそらく

súperman.
超人

　　○「そんなことができる人は超人を除いてまずいない」
　　　→「できるのは超人だけ」という意味になる

- not ... everything（すべてが…というわけではない）〈部分否定〉
- no ... except ～（～以外は…でない）〈二重否定〉

(On the other hand), don't say / you're hopeless, or there's
その一方，その反面　　　　　　　　　　　　　　　　　　　　　～しても無駄だ

no use in trying. Nobody is perfect; / but nobody is

hopeless, either.
　　　　もまた（～でない）

- not ... you're hopeless（望みがないと言うな）〈二重否定〉
- there's no use (in) ～ing（～しても無駄だ）
- nobody ... is hopeless（望みがない者はだれもいない）〈二重否定〉
　　　　　　　　　　　　（→みんな望みがある）
- not ..., either（…もまた…でない）〈肯定文なら too, also〉

〔解答〕 すべてにおいてうまくやる必要はない。そんなことができる人はまずいない，おそらく超人を除けば。その反面，「望みがない」とか「やってもむだだ」とか言ってはならない。完全な人はいないが，望みがない人もいないのだから。

「だれにでも望みはある」という意味

第15回 否定

3 次の日本文を英語に訳しなさい。

(1) 私の父はいっさい酒を飲まない。兄もそうだ。
　　　　　　　　　not ... at all

My father [does not drink at all. / never drinks,] [Nor does my brother. (V S) / My brother doesn't (drink), either.]

→ 否定文なので So V + S. ではない
（Neither + V + S）
（too ではない）

- **not ... at all**（まったく…でない）
- **not ..., nor V + S**（…でないが，～もまた…でない）
- **.... So V + S.**（…だが，～もそうだ）
  - He smokes. So do I.
  - He does not smoke. Nor do I.
- **not ..., either.**（～もまた…でない）
  - 「～もまた」は肯定文の場合は too

(2) そんなつまらぬ話題に関心のある人はほとんどいないだろう。
　　　　　　　　　　　　　　　　　　　　　　few を用いる

such [an unimportant subject / a dull topic / a trifling matter] など

be interested in ～
have an interest in ～

- **few**（ほとんどない）⇔ **a few**（いくらかの，少しの）
  - Few people will ...
- **hardly any ～**（ほとんどだれも～しない）
  - Hardly any people will ...

(3) 今日では（私たちの日常の会話の中に）英語の2つや3つ使われないことはめったにない。

- in our everyday talk / daily conversation
- a few English words
- 「通例使われている」という意味
- seldom, rarely

Today [we usually use / it seldom happens that we don't use] a few English words in our everyday talk.

- **seldom / rarely**（めったに～しない）
- **hardly / scarcely**（ほとんど～しない）

(4)（私たちのまわりには），おもしろい読み物がたくさんあるが，/ すべてが私たちを向上させてくれるとは限らない。

- around us
- a lot of interesting books
- help us improve ourselves
- not all of them ... ［部分否定］

[主語を変えれば
we cannot always [improve ourselves by reading them / be the better for reading them]]

- **not all ... / not every ～**（すべてが…とは限らない）
  Not all books are instructive.
  Not every book is instructive.

第15回 否定

(5) 人生はくり返しがきかないので，(何事をするにも) 細心にすぎることはない。

- we cannot live our life once again
- our life cannot be repeated

in doing anything

○ we cannot be too careful
（いくら注意してもいい）

- **cannot ... too ～**（どんなに～してもしすぎではない）　いくら～しても
- **cannot ... enough**（どんなに～しても十分ではない）　いいくらいだ
  I can't thank you enough.

〔解答〕
(1) My father doesn't drink at all. Nor does my brother.
(2) Few people will be interested in such a trifling subject.
(3) Today it seldom happens that our daily conversations do not contain a few English words.
(4) We find a lot of interesting books around us, / but not all of them help us (to) improve ourselves.
(5) We cannot live our life once again, / so we cannot be too careful in doing anything.

第 16 回

接 続 詞

単語と単語
句と句　　などをつなぐ
節と節
文と文

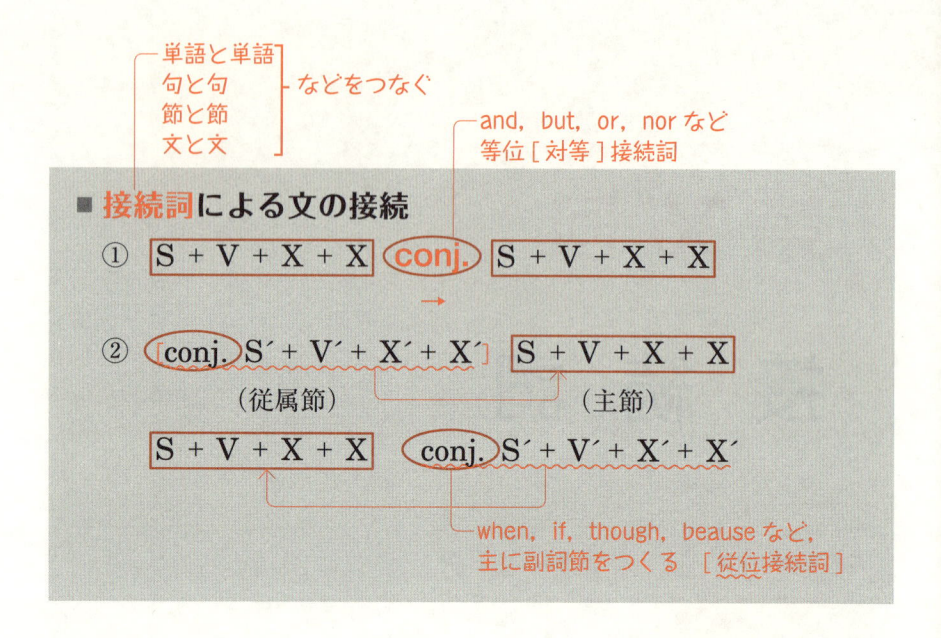

and, but, or, nor など
等位［対等］接続詞

■ **接続詞**による文の接続

① S + V + X + X (conj.) S + V + X + X

② (conj.) S´ + V´ + X´ + X´　S + V + X + X
　　　　　（従属節）　　　　　（主節）

　S + V + X + X　(conj.) S´ + V´ + X´ + X´

when, if, though, beause など，
主に副詞節をつくる［従位接続詞］

TRACK 01

1 （　）内から最も適当なものを選び，○で囲みなさい。

(1) Stop eating candy, /（and, if, **or**, unless）you'll make
　　　　　　　　　　　　　　　　　　　　　　　　　　　　V
yourself ill.
　O　　C
　　　　　　　　さもないと（ótherwise）
　　　　　　　　　　　　　（if not …）

If you don't stop eating candy, you'll … とほぼ同じ意味

- … and …（…そして…）
  - 命令文 … and …（→ If …）（…しなさい，そうすれば…）
  - 命令文 … or …（→ If … not …）（…しなさい，さもないと…）
- … but …（しかし…，けれども…）（and yet）
  … so …（そこで…，したがって…）

(2) I do<u>n't</u> have any money, / (either, neither, **nor**, so) <u>do</u> <u>I</u>
   <u>have</u> <u>any credit cards</u>.
   V   O   また〜でもない   S

倒置が起こる。I'm not rich, nor do I wish to be (rich).

- not ..., nor V + S. ⎫ (...でない, また
- not .... Neither V + S. ⎭   [〜も] 〜でない)

  I don't have ..., nor do I have 〜.

  You don't like it. ⎧ Nor do I.
                    ⎨ Neither do I.
                    ⎩ And I don't, either.

(3) Mr. Jones <u>is satisfied</u> / (**that**, though, what, with) all of
              …に満足している
              [with the fact]
   his students passed his test.

- **be satisfied that ...**（…に満足している）
  be surprised that ...（…に驚く）
- **be glad that ...**（…をうれしく思う）
  be sorry that ...（…を残念に思う）
  I'm sorry that you failed the test.

209

(4) Mrs. Ford hasn't made up her mind (about, how, when, <u>whether</u>) to buy the house <u>or not</u>.

まだ決心していない

家を買うべきかどうか

(whether she should buy the house or not)

- whether to ～ or not（～すべきかどうか）
  how to ～
  what to ～
  when to ～

(5) [(After, During, Stayed, While) in Europe], I visited a lot of art galleries.

During my stay in Europe — Staying in Europe

[I was] を省略できる

たくさんの

美術館

- while (I was) in Europe（ヨーロッパにいる間）
  when (I was) a child（子どもだった頃）
  if (it is) necessary（必要ならば）
  　　└ 省略可能

(6) It's very nice to see you again. It's been more than three years [(after, from, (since), when) we last met], hasn't it?

この前(最後に)会って以来(3年以上になるね)
「久しぶりだね」It's been ages (since I met you last).
　　　　　　　　　　　　　(since we last met).

- since ... (…して以来)
- it is ～
  it has been ～ } since ... (…してから～になる)
  ～ have passed

  Ten years have passed since he died.
  He has been dead for ten years.

前置詞句(＋名詞)
…だけれども　　　　　　　　　　　グループのほぼ半分が病気になったので
(7) [(Although, Because of, For, (Since)) nearly half the group became sick], the plan had to be cancelled.
　　　　　　　　　　　　　　　　　　　中止され(なければならなかった)

- since ... (…であるから[には]) 〈理由を表す〉
  通例文頭で　　Since he is ill, we can't take him with us.
- as ... (…なので)
- ... because ... (…なので，なぜなら…だから)
- ..., for ... (というのは…だからだ)

TRACK 03

(8) I won't help my sister <u>any more</u> [(but, except, (unless), without) she <u>begs me</u>].
　　　　　　　　　　　　もうこれ以上〜しない　　　〜でない限り
　　　　　　　　　　　　もはや〜しない　　　　　　except when ...
　　　　　　　　　　　　　　　　　　　　　　　　(if ... not 〜に近い)
　[ぜひにと]頼む

- **unless** ...（…でない限り，…の場合以外には）
　　　　　（もし…でないならば）if ... not 〜に近い

(9) You may keep the book [(as far as, (as long as), though, until) you don't soil it].
　　　　　　　　　　　　　　　汚さない限りは←汚さないうちは(while)

- **as long as ... / so long as ...**（[時間的に]…である限り）
- **as far as ... / so far as ...**（[程度が]…である限り）
　as far as I know（私の知る限り）
　so far as I am concerned（私に関する限り）

(10) What a stupid fellow he is (as, because, since, (that)) he <u>should get angry</u> (at such trifles)!
　　　　　　　　　　　　　　　　　　　　　　　　　　〜に腹を立てる　こんな細かなこと，つまらないこと

- **that ... should 〜**（…が〜するとは，〜するなんて）
　　　　　　　　　　意外な感じ，驚きの感じ

〔解答〕
(1) **or**　　(2) **nor**　　(3) **that**　　(4) **whether**　　(5) **While**
(6) **since**　(7) **Since**　(8) **unless**　(9) **as long as**　(10) **that**

第16回 接続詞

TRACK 04

2 それぞれ意味の通る文になるように，[ ]内の語を並べ換えなさい。文頭の語は大文字で書き始めること。

(1) I stayed on [fear, feel, for, he, lonely, might].
I stayed on [for fear he might feel lonely.]
そのまま　　　　[lest he should feel lonely.
とどまった　　　　so that he might not feel lonely.]

> ■ 副詞節を導く接続詞
> when ..., as ...
> if ..., though ... 以外にもいろいろある
> ● for fear ... may[should] ~
>   lest ... should ~ 　　　　(…が~するといけないから)
> ● so that ... may not ~　(…が~しないように)
>   so
>   that

(2) I felt as [been, had, I, if, nose, on, punched, the].
I felt as if I had been punched on the nose.
　　　　　　鼻をなぐられたかのように感じた

> ● as if ... / as though ... （まるで…であるかのように）
>   └ 仮定法の動詞が通常使われる
> ● punch me on the nose（私の鼻にパンチをくらわす）
>   strike me on the head（私の頭をなぐる）
>   catch me by the arm（私の腕をつかむ）
>   look me in the face（私の顔を見る）

(3) [hard, however, may, try, you], it will be impossible to finish the work in a day.

[However hard you may try], it will be impossible to finish the work in a day.
　└ hard は however の直後に

「どんなにいっしょうけんめいやってみても…」

However rich he [may be, ...
　　　　　　　　 [is, ...
（どんなに金持ちであっても…）

- **however** [＋ 形容詞・副詞] ... may 〜（どんなに〜しても）
- **no matter how** ... may 〜（どのように〜しても）

in a low voice（低い声で）

(4) Professor Stout spoke [a, in, low, such, that, voice] none of us could hear him.

Professor Stout spoke [in such a low voice that none of us could hear him.
　　　　　　　　　　　[in so low a voice that ...
　　　　　　　　　　　 （語順の相違に注意）

名詞を含む（in such a loud voice that ...）

- **such** ... that ... ｝（あまり…なので…）
  so ... that ...

  形容詞・副詞（so loudly that ...）

  He works { so diligently   } that ...（あまり勤勉に働くので…）
            { with such diligence }

  形と語順に注意！

第16回 接続詞

TRACK 05

(5) The roof had fallen in, / [cóttage, inhábitable, not, so, the, that, was].
くずれて落ち込んでいた　　住める（住みつく + -able）
山荘，小屋

The roof had fallen in, so that the cottage was not inhábitable.
したがって，その結果　　（住めなくなった）

- ..., so that ...
- ..., so ... / ..., and so ... 　（…そこで[それゆえ，したがって]…）
  └ thérefore（それゆえに）

(6) [had, him, no, políceman, sooner, stopped, the] than he started running away.

No sooner had the políceman stopped him than he started running away.
　　　　　└ ここに倒置が起きる
「警官が彼を止めたとたんに，彼は逃げ出した」
　　　　　(V + S)

- **No sooner ... than ...**（…するやいなや～）
  No sooner had I come in than the telephone rang.
  （入るやいなや電話が鳴った）
- **As soon as ～, ...**（～するとすぐに…）
  The moment ～, ...（～したとたんに…）
- **Hardly ... when[before] ～**
  Scarcely ... when[before] ～　（…するかしないかのうちにもう…）
  Hardly had I come in when ...

(7) John wrote pássionate letters to Mary [doing, every, felt, he, like, so, time].

情熱的な ... feel like ～ing（～したくなる）

John wrote pássionate letters to Mary / every time he felt like doing so.　(whenever)

そうしたくなったときはいつでも
そうしたくなるたびに

> ● every time ...（…するたびごとに）
> whenever ...（…のときはいつでも）

(8) No more desk plan will do, [be, concéived, how, ingéniously, it, matter, may, no].

机上のプランではもはやだめだろう
巧妙に

役に立つ，間に合う，結構だ
Any time after three will do.
「3時以後ならいつでもいいですよ」

No more desk plan will do, no matter how ingéniously concéived it may be.

どんなに巧みに練られていようとも

> ● no matter how [+ 形容詞・副詞] ... may ～　　(どんなに…が～
> 　 however [+ 形容詞・副詞] ... may ～　　　　　　であろうとも)
>
> 　no matter how　　} beautifully dressed she may be, ...
> 　however
>
> （どんなにきれいに着飾っても）
>
> ● no matter who may ～　　} (だれが～であろうとも)
> 　 whoever may ～

- no matter what (...) may 〜
  whatever (...) may 〜 } (何が[何を] 〜であろうとも)

  no matter what
  whatever } others may say, ...　他人が何と言おうと…

- no matter where ... may 〜
  wherever ... may 〜 } (どこで〜しようとも)

〔解答〕
(1) I stayed on <u>for fear he might feel lonely.</u>
(2) I felt as <u>if I had been punched on the nose.</u>
(3) <u>However hard you may try</u>, it will be impossible to finish the work in a day.
(4) Professor Stout spoke <u>in such a low voice that</u> none of us could hear him.
(5) The roof had fallen in, <u>so that the cottage was not inhabitable.</u>
(6) <u>No sooner had the policeman stopped him</u> than he started running away.
(7) John wrote passionate letters to Mary <u>every time he felt like doing so.</u>
(8) No more desk plan will do, <u>no matter how ingeniously conceived it may be.</u>

TRACK 06

3 次の日本文を( )内の語を用いて英語に訳しなさい。

(1) 歯をみがいてから寝なさい。(before)
　　tooth(単数形), teeth(複数形)
　→寝る前に歯を磨きなさい

<u>Brush your teeth before you go to bed.</u>
(Go to bed after you brush your teeth.)

- **before** ...（…の前に）
- **after** ...（…の後に）　　あたりまえの副詞節

(2) ちょっと留守にしたすきに，どろぼうに入られた。(**robbed**)
　　be out for a moment

rob の使い方を復習しておくとよい
[rob A of B (A から B)
[A is robbed of B. (A は B を)

<u>While I was out for a moment, I had my house robbed.</u>
　　　　S　V　　O　　　　C

(my house was robbed [by someone] という意味が含まれる)

- **while** ...（…する間に）
　while I was in Europe（ヨーロッパにいる間に）

第16回 接続詞

(3) ただ貧しいからといって人を軽蔑してはいけない。(simply)

despise, disdain
look down on (～を見下す)

Do not / Never
You should(not) despise a man simply because he is poor.
others just[only] because they are poor.

- not ... (simply) because ～ (～だからといって…してはいけない)

She did (not) come because she wanted to see me.

(○)「私に会いたいから来たわけではない」
　　notは because ... 以下も含めて否定する！
(×)「彼女は来なかった，なぜなら私に会いたかったから」(!?)

(4) 私は [ファックスを受け取るとすぐ] 彼の事務所へ電話をかけた。(soon)

As soon as
Soon after] I received his fax,

　　　　　　　　　　I telephoned his office.

- as soon as ... (…するとすぐに)
  soon after ... (…する直後に)
- the moment ... (…する[した]瞬間に)

219

(5) 彼は，[立ち去るところを人に見られないように]（暗くなるまで）待っていた。(leave)

be seen to 〜（← see ＋ O ＋ 原形不定詞）

$$\left[\begin{array}{l}\text{lest} \\ \text{for fear}\end{array}\right] \text{he should be seen to leave.}$$
$$\text{so (that) he might not be seen to leave.}$$

この副詞節が要点

He waited till it was dark lest he should be seen to leave.

- till ... / until ...（…するまで）
- for fear ... should / may 〜
  lest ... should 〜 ｝（…が〜するといけないから）
- so (that) ... may not 〜
  (so) that ... may not 〜 ｝（…が〜しないように）

〔解答〕
(1) Brush your teeth before you go to bed.
(2) While I was out for a moment, I had my house robbed.
(3) You should not despise a man simply because he is poor.
(4) As soon as I received his fax, I telephoned his office.
(5) He waited till it was dark lest he should be seen to leave. / He waited till dark so he might not be seen to leave.

第16回　接続詞

4 下線部に注意して，次の英文を日本語に訳しなさい。

It is not the number of books (which a young man reads) that makes him intelligent and well informed, / but the number of well-chosen ones (that he has mastered.)

- V: makes
- O: him
- C: intelligent and well informed
- 知的で博識の
- mastered: マスターする，完全に理解する

(×)「しかし…」
ここを誤らないのが最大の要点
(○) not A but B（A ではなくて B）

- **It is ... that ～.** という強調構文
- **not A but B** と対応する
  ◎「若者を知的で博識にしてくれるのは A ではなくて，B のほうだ」という骨組みをつかむ！

  ここを強める強調構文
- **it is not A but B / that ....**
  → it is not A that ... / but B.
  （…なのは A ではなく B だ）
  この but を誤りやすいので特に注意！

〔解答〕　若者を知的で博識にしてくれるのは，読む本の数ではなくて，精選された書物をどれだけ完全に自分のものとしたかである。

第17回

前置詞

■ **前置詞のはたらき**

S + V + X + X のどこでも **prep.** + N

文中に「前置詞＋名詞」の形が現れる

- 形容詞の働き
- 副詞の働き
- 前置詞の後にも現れる

  from behind the curtain（カーテンの後ろから）

■ **前置詞句を含む慣用語句**

- 動詞との結びつき　depend on, look at [into / over / on など]
- 形容詞との結びつき

  be conscious of / be aware of など

- 群前置詞（1つの前置詞の働き）

  by means of, in spite of など

TRACK 01

1 （　）内の日本語を参考にして，空所に適当な前置詞を入れなさい。

(1) Can you tell the ass (from) the pony?　（区別する）
　　　　　　　　　　　ろば　　　　　　　　ポニー（小型の馬）

- tell A from B / know A from B
- distinguish A from B / distinguish between A and B
  区別する

（AとBを区別する）

(2) She is always dressed (in) white. （服を着ている）
　　　　　　　　　　　　　　　白い服

- **be dressed in ～**
　　　～を身につけて，（帽子を）かぶって，（靴を）はいて
- **have ～ on**
　She has a miniskirt on.　──副詞（前置詞ではない）
　She is dressed in a miniskirt.　You look very nice in that dress.
　　　　　　　　　　　　　　　　（あのドレスとても似合ってるわよ）

(3) I became acquáinted with Meg (through) Mr. Scriver.
　　～と知り合いになった　　　　　　　　～を通じて　　（～の紹介で）

- **be acquáinted with ～**（～と知り合いである）
- **through**（～を貫いて，～を通して）
　through a travel agent
　（旅行代理店を通じて）
　He got a job through my help.
　（私の助けで仕事についた）

(4) Payment will be made (on) delivery. （配達されしだい）
　　支払い

- **on delivery**（配達されるとすぐに）
　on request（請求がありしだい）
- **on ～ing**（～するとすぐに）
　on hearing the news
　（知らせを聞くとすぐに）
　(as soon as I heard the news)

(5) We'll pay you $20 ((for)) your service.（サービス代として）
「〜と引きかえに」という感じ

- **pay A (for) B / buy B (for) A**（B の代金として A を支払う）
  「〜と交換に」という感じ

  I paid 20 dollars for it.
  I bought it at 20 dollars.
  I got it for 20 dollars.

(6) She always buys milk ((by)) the gallon.（ガロン単位で）
the にも注意

- **by the gallon**（ガロン単位で）
  by the pound（ポンド単位で）
    Sugar is sold by the pound.
    They sell sugar by the pound.（1 ポンドいくらで売る）
- **by the hour**（1 時間いくらで）
  by the month（月単位で，1 か月いくらで）
    be paid ⎰ by the week（週給で）
           ⎱ by the month（月給で）

～以外の
(7) He eats nothing (but) fruit (for breakfast).
    〜だけしか(only)   朝食に   （果物だけしか）

- **nothing but 〜**（〜だけ，〜しか）(only 〜)
- **for breakfast**（朝食に）
    for lunch, for supper, for dinner
    What would you like for dessert?（デザートは何にしますか）

(8) You can't master English ((in)) a month or two.)
(for はダメ！)　　　　　　　　　　（1，2か月で）

- **in** a month or two （1，2か月のうちに，1，2か月後に）
  for a month or two （1，2か月間，1，2か月にわたって）

(9) He visited some temples ((during) his stay in Kyoto).
　　　　　　　　　　　　　　　　　　　　　（滞在中に）

- **during** ～（〜の間［じゅう，ずっと］）〈前置詞〉
  while ...（…する間）〈接続詞〉
  while he was staying in Kyoto

(10) I haven't seen Tom (since) two weeks ago.
　　　　　　　　 for two weeks.　　　（2週間前から）
　　　　　　　　 these two weeks.　　（from はダメ！）

- **have p.p. ... since** ～（〜以来…）
  完了形とともに使うのが普通
  前置詞にも接続詞にも｛ since 2001
  　　　　　　　　　　　 since he was born in 2001

(11) Don't cross the street ((against) a red light). （無視して）

- **against** ～（〜にさからって，よりかかって，ぶつかって，反対して）
  　　　　　　　　　　　　　　　　└という感じ
- **against** （〜に反対して）⇔ **for** （〜に賛成して）
- **lean against** ～（［壁など］によりかかる）

(12) The score now is two (**to**) nothing. （2 対 0）

> ● **A to B**（A 対 B）
> We won with[by] a score of 5 to 3. （5 － 3 のスコアで）
> The exchange rate is 100 yen to 1 dollar.
> 　　　（変換レートは 1 ドル 100 円です）

(13) You should **never fail to** be there ((**by**) seven). （7 時までに）
　　　　　　　　必ず～する(be sure to)　till ではない！

> ● by ～ （～までに）［期限］
> till, until ～ （［継続して］～まで）
> 　come by seven（7 時までに来る）
> 　wait till seven（7 時まで待つ）　｝区別せよ ○
> ● 時を表す前置詞：at, in, on, by, since, during, …など
> ● 場所を表す前置詞：at, in, on, over, under, above, beneath, …
> 　　　　　　　　　 など

(14) He **died** suddenly (**of**) heart failure. （心臓まひで）
　　　　　　　　　　　～が原因で

> ● die of ～ / die from ～ （～で死ぬ）
> 　　　｜　　　　　　｜
> 　cancer(ガンで)　overwork(過労で)

第17回　前置詞

(15) I want to make up (for) lost time.（埋め合わせる）
　　　　　　　　　～をつぐなう，～を取り返す

- **make up for**（～を補う，～の埋め合わせをする）
  make up は「作り上げる，補う」という感じ
  make up one's face（化粧する）
  make up a story（お話をでっちあげる）などなど

(16) I am convinced (of) these facts.（確信する）

- **be convinced of ~**（～を確信している）
- **convince A of B**（A に B を納得させる）

まとめて1つの前置詞とみなす

(17) Thoughts are expressed ((by) means of words).
　　　思想　　　　　　　　　　　　　　　　　　（言葉によって）

- **by means of ~**（～を使って，～を手段にして）

あれだけの富 [の割には／を考えても]

(18) (For all his wealth), he is not at all happy.（裕福なのに）
　　　[With]　　　　　　　　　　　全然～でない
　　　あれだけの富がありながら

- **for all ~**（[あれだけの] ～を考えてみても → ～ にもかかわらず）
  for his age（年齢の割には，年齢を考えると）
- **with all ~**（[あれだけの] ～をもってしても）

229

(19) He <u>took</u> me (by) <u>the arm</u> / and made me walk with him.

arm と hand は？
leg と foot は？

（腕を取る）

「私をつかんだ，腕のところを」という言い方
　［本体］　　　　［部分］

- take ... (by) the arm（…の腕をとる）
  grab ... (by) the sleeve（…のそでをつかむ）
- look ... <u>in</u> the face（…の顔を見る）
- punch ... <u>on</u> the nose（…の鼻をなぐる）
  pat ... <u>on</u> the shoulder（…の肩を叩く）
  kiss ... <u>on</u> the lips（…のくちびるにキスをする）

(20) I have nothing more to say ((as) <u>to</u> this question).
　　これ以上言うことはない

（〜について）

- 群前置詞の例
  <u>as to</u> 〜（〜について，〜に関して）
  　（about 〜 / on 〜 / concérning 〜）
  in respect of / with respect to
  as regards / with réference to 〜（〜に関して）
  As for myself, ...
  　私はどうかと言えば（as[so] far as I am concérned）
  　　He's for the idea. But <u>as for</u> myself I'm against it.
  　　（彼はその考えに賛成よ。でも私はどうかと言うと反対だわ）
  〈参考〉As far as the passivizability of this verb is concerned, ...
  　　（この動詞が受動態にできるかどうかに関して言うと，…）

〔解答〕
(1) **from**　(2) **in**　(3) **through**　(4) **on**　(5) **for**　(6) **by**
(7) **but**　(8) **in**　(9) **during**　(10) **since**　(11) **against**　(12) **to**
(13) **by**　(14) **of**　(15) **for**　(16) **of**　(17) **by**　(18) **For**
(19) **by**　(20) **as**

TRACK 03

■ 頻出する前置詞の慣用法

2 次の各組の英文がほぼ同じ意味になるように，空所に適当な前置詞を入れなさい。

(1) What has happened to John?
　= What has become (of) John?

> ● **What has become of ~?**（~はどうなったか）
> What has he become? — (He has become) A teacher. とは異なる

(2) I tried again / but did not succeed.
　= I tried again / (without) success.
　　試みたが[その結果]成功しなかった
　　(×)「成功せずに試みた」

> ● **without success**（[結果は]成功しなかった）
> **in vain / without avail / to no avail**（[結果は]むだだった）
> ● **only to fail**（[結果は]失敗した）

(3) Some objected to our plan.
　　　~に反対した
　= Some were (against) our plan.
　　　　　　~に反対だった

> ● **against**（~に反対して）
> **for**（~に賛成して）

(4) He is mad with anger.
　　= He is (beside) himself with anger.
　　　　　　　怒りで逆上している
　　　　　　　我を忘れて

- **beside oneself with ~**（~で我を忘れて，逆上して）
  └ その他 for oneself, by oneself, to oneself は？

(5) You need not pay for it.
　　　　　　　　　~の代金を払う
　　= You can have it (for) nothing.
　　　　　　　　　　　　　　無料で

- **for nothing / free (of charge)**（無料で，ただで）

(6) She said, "Can I have the photo?"
　　= She asked (for) the photo. （写真をほしがった）
　　　　　　　求めて，ほしがって

- **ask for ~**（[物]をほしがる，要求する）

(7) He did not know what to say.
　　= He was at a loss (for) words.
　　　　　　途方にくれた　　　~を求めて，探して

「何と言っていいか（わからず）困ってしまった」

- **be at a loss for ~**（~を求めて途方にくれる）
  その他 look for ~ / search for ~ / call for ~ / send for ~ など，
  　　　　　　　　　　　　　　　for の感じをつかんでおく

233

(8) Would you like another cup?
 = Would you care (for) another cup ?
 もう一杯いかがですか

- **care for ~**（~を好む）(like) —疑問文・否定文で
   He didn't care for dancing.
   (ダンスは好きではなかった)
- **care for ~**（~の世話をする）(look after)

著者の名前
(9) The author's name is famíliar to us.　　(←物が主語)
 = We are familiar (with) the author's name.　(←人が主語)
  ~になじみがある

- **A is famíliar to B.**（A は B に知られている）
  B is familiar with A.（B は A を知っている）

(10) I felt pity [when I saw the poor children.]
 = I felt pity [(at) the sight of the poor children.]
   ~を見て

- **at the sight of ~**（~を見て）
- **at first sight**（一見して，一目で）
   fall in love with her at first sight
   (彼女に一目惚れする)

第17回 前置詞

(11) [When Nancy heard the sad news], she began to cry.
= [(On) hearing the sad news], Nancy began to cry.

- on ～ing（～するとすぐに）（→ when / as soon as …）

(12) He failed repéatedly, / but he never gave up.
　　　くり返し，何度も　　　　　　　あきらめなかった
= He never gave up ((in) spite (of) his repeated failures).
　　　　　　　　　though he failed repeatedly.

- in spite of ～ / despite ～（～にもかかわらず）
  in spite of { his wound（負傷したにもかかわらず）
  　　　　　　 his illness（病気にもめげずに）

(13) My uncle gave me a watch as well as a cámera.
= My uncle gave me a watch / (in) addition (to) a camera.
　　　　　　　　　　　　　　カメラに加えて（時計もくれた）

- in addition to ～ / besides ～ / on top of ～（～に加えて）
- B as well as A（AばかりかBも）(not only A but B)

(14) She didn't stay at home, / but she went out.
= ((Instead) (of) staying at home), she went out.
　　家にいる代わりに，家にいないで

- instead of ～（～の代わりに，～しないで）
- not A but B（AではなくてB）

235

(15) The name of the person (responsible for our new project) will soon be announced.　～に責任がある　　新しいプロジェクト(計画)

= The name of the person (in) charge (of) our new plan) will soon be announced.　～を担当している
発表されるだろう　　　　　　　　　　　～の責任者である

- **in charge of ～**（～を担当している，～の責任がある）
- **be responsible for ～**（～に対して責任がある）

〔解答〕
(1) **of**　　(2) **without**　(3) **against**　(4) **beside**　(5) **for**
(6) **for**　 (7) **for**　　　(8) **for**　　 (9) **with**　 (10) **at**
(11) **On**　 (12) **in, of**　 (13) **in, to**　(14) **Instead of**　(15) **in, of**

第17回　前置詞

TRACK 04

■ 前置詞の有無など

3 次の文中の空所に前置詞が必要ならばその前置詞を，不必要ならば×を書き入れなさい。

Get on the bus <u>for</u> the station. [When it <u>approaches</u> (1)(×)
～行きの，～へ向かう　　　　　～に近づく（come near）
　　　　　　　　　　　　他動詞なので approach to ～（×）
　　　　　　　　　　　　to は不要！

the station], you will see a big fountain (2)(on) <u>your left</u>).
　　　　　　　　　　　　　　泉，噴水

The hotel (you <u>are speaking</u> (3)(of)) is <u>near</u> (4)(×) this
　　　　　　　　　　　　　　　　　　　（～に近い）
　　　　　　　　　　　　　　　　　　　near to ～（×）ではなく
　　　　　　　　　　　　　　　　　　　near ～でよい

fountain, / so you will <u>have no trouble</u> <u>locating</u> it.
　　　　　　　　　　　　～するのに手間は　　[場所を]つきとめる
　　　　　　　　　　　　かからない

● 前置詞が不要な他動詞　←日本語に注意！
　appróach（～に近づく）
　leave（～から出発する）(start from)
　reach（～に着く）
　atténd（～に通う，～に出席する）
　marry（～と結婚する）(get married to)
　enter（～に入る）
　mention（～について言う）(talk about)
　discúss（～について議論する）(talk over)
　resémble（～と[～に]似ている）(look like)

- **on** one's **left**（左側に）**/ to** one's **left**（左のほうに）
- **speak of / talk of / speak about** ～（～について話す）
- **near** ～（[前置詞として] ～の近くに）— **near to** ～の to は不要！
   His office is very near to the bank.— 形容詞としては near to ～
- **nearer to** ～ **/ nearest to** ～
   　　　　　　　　　　　—[形容詞として]比較級・最上級で to を使う
   nearest to the door（ドアにいちばん近い）

　　　　　　　　　　　　　　　　　than ではない！
The hotél is not inférior (5)(to) any first-class hotel (6)((in) the world), / and they will take care (7)(of) all your
　　　　　　　　　　　　　　　　いっさい個人的な必要，面倒をみてくれる
personal needs, free (8)(of) charge. Moreover, [if you turn right at the corner], you will find the Central Post Office (9)(×) [which is (10)(at) your service (twenty hours a day)].
　　　　　　　　　S′　V′　　C′　あなたの役に立つ　　1日24時間いつでも
　　　　　　　　　　　　　　　利用できる
　　　　　主格の関係代名詞
　　　（← It is at your service ...）
in which ではない！

- **inférior to**（～より劣る）
  supérior to（～よりすぐれている）　　　　} **than** を使わない比較表現の例
- **senior to**（～より年上）
  junior to（～より年下）
- **take care of**（～の面倒をみる）

第17回　前置詞

- **free of charge / for nothing**（無料で，ただで）
- **at one's service**（～の役に立つ）〈形容詞句〉
  I'm always at your service.
  （いつでもお役に立ちます→何なりと申しつけてください）
- **at one's disposal**（～が自由に処分できる，～の意のままである）
  This money is at my disposal.
  （この金は私の自由になる）

〔解答〕
(1) × (2) on (3) of (4) × (5) to
(6) in (7) of (8) of (9) × (10) at

TRACK 05

4 下線部に特に注意して，次の英文を日本語に訳せ。

[In spite of the love of the parents for their child and their fears for her safety], they both knew / that their daughter was an incredibly stupid, dull little girl. This knowledge only added to their fears.

～にもかかわらず　親が子供をかわいがること
親が娘の安全を心配すること
信じられないほど　愚かな　鈍い(頭がよくない)
～を増す(increase)　(×)この知識は…
(○)これを知っているがために…
これがわかっているために…

(×)「両親の彼らの子供に対する愛情と彼女の安全に対する彼らの心配にもかかわらず…」ただ名詞・前置詞をたどるだけではだめ！

(○)→ Though the parents loved their child and feared for her safety, …

- **the love of A for B**（AのBへの愛 → AがBを愛する気持ち）
  (S')　(O')
- **one's fears for ～**（…の～への心配 → …が～を心配すること）
  (S')　　(O')

〔解答〕　両親はわが子を可愛がっていて，その子が無事に育つようにいろいろ気をつかってはいたけれども，/ その娘が信じられぬほど愚かで頭の悪い少女であることを2人とも知っていた。それがわかっているために，2人の心配はなお増すばかりだった。

第 18 回

出題形式別・実戦問題演習（1）

TRACK 01

《選択完成問題》

1 各文の空所を補うのに最も適当な語を(A)〜(K)から選びなさい。同じ語をくり返し使ってもよい。また，空所に何も補う必要のない場合には(L)を選びなさい。

(A) at　(B) by　(C) for　(D) from　(E) in　(F) into
(G) of　(H) on　(I) to　(J) under　(K) with　(L) NO WORD

(1) "When will her plane be arriving ×?" "I have no idéa."

　　　　　　　　　　　　　　　　　自動詞　at, in は不要
　　　　　　　　　　　　　　　　　　　　　　　　　　わからない

- arrive at 〜（[ある地点]に到着する）
  arrive in 〜（[比較的広い場所]に到着する）

  arrive at Narita Airport
  arrive in Tokyo　　　　　　　という感じ

(2) The cúrrency exchánge rate (of nearly 100 yen **to** the dollar) was históric.
　　　　　　　通貨の交換レート　　　　　　　A to B(A 対 B)
　　　　　　　　　　　　　　　　歴史的な

- the exchange rate of A to B（A 対 B の[通貨]交換レート）
- with a score of A to B（A 対 B のスコアで）
  win with[by] a score of 4 to 1（4 対 1 で勝つ）

242

(3) The chain store tried to earn exceptionally high prófits (at the cost of consúmers).
　　異常に　　高い利益
　　at ～ 消費者を犠牲にして
　　→「チェーンストアが異常なほど高い利益を得ようとした結果，消費者が犠牲になった」

- **at the cost of ～ / at the expense of ～**
  (～の代償[費用]で，～を犠牲にして)
- **at all cost(s) / at any cost**
  (どんなに犠牲[代償]を払っても→ぜひとも) (at any price)
  prevent war at all costs (なんとしても戦争を回避する)

(4) I think I'm safe in saying / that everyone will be (for) our propósal.
　　…と言っても大丈夫だと思う　　～に賛成している
　　提案 < propose(提案する)　　(反対は against ～)

- **for ～ / in favor of ～** (～に賛成して)
- **against ～ / in opposition to ～** (～に反対して)

(5) You can contact him by telephone, (anytime / between 9 a.m. and 5 p.m.)
　　～と連絡をとる

- **by telephone** (電話で[連絡する])
  over the telephone (電話で[話す])
  on the telephone (電話で，電話に出ている)
  　I spoke to her on[over] the telephone. (電話で話した)
  　She is on the telephone. (電話中です)

- by car / by bus / by ship など
  →冠詞をつけない場合（〜を利用して）
- between A and B（AとBとの間に）

(6) The call (for stricter anti-pollútion contróls) remains unheard.

〜を求める感じ！
もっと厳しい汚染の抑制
V
いまだ聞かれない
C

- call for 〜 / ask for 〜（〜を要求する）
  look for 〜 / search for 〜（〜を探す）

(7) Fans (in their teens and early 20s) rushed (toward the stage).
10代と20代前半の

- in one's teens（[13〜19歳の]十代の）
  in one's twenties（20代に）
  She's still in her ｛ early thirties.（まだ30代前半だ）
  　　　　　　　　　 late teens.（まだ10代後半だ）

(8) He jumped into the river / and saved the little girl from drowning.
少女を溺れるのから救った

- save A from B（AをBから救う）

244

(9) "Is there anything (I can help you with)?" "Yes, I'm looking for a man (called Allan White)."
　　　　　　　　　　　　　　　　　　　　　～を探している

> 「～に関して」という感じ
>
> ● help A with B（AのBを助ける）
>   Could you help ｛ me with ｛ this translation?（この翻訳を…）
>   　　　　　　　　　　　　　　 this assignment?（この宿題を…）
>   　　　　　　　　my translation?（×）

(10) The man worked far into the night (to buy the house for his family).
　　　　　　　　　　　　　夜ふけまで

> ● far into the night / late into the night（夜ふけまで）
>   ～の中へ，～の中まで(in ＋ to) — dive into the water（水中へもぐる）

TRACK 02

(11) To say he was ignorant of the ways of the world / is no excuse.
　　　S　　　　 ～を知らない　　世間の習慣　　　　　 V C
　　　　　　　　　　　　　　　　世のならわし
　　…は言い訳にはならない

> ● be ignorant of ～（～を知らない）
>   be aware of ～（～に気づいている，知っている）
>   be conscious of ～（～を意識している）
>   　　スペリングに注意。sを落とさない！
> ● be sure of / be convinced of（～を確信している）

(12) [When the earthquake hit], all the pictures (on the wall)
　　 地震が発生したとき…　　　　　　　　　　　　　壁(の上)にかかっていた
fell to the floor.

> - **on the wall**（壁に）
>   **on the ceiling**（天井に）
>   壁や天井でも on
>   on は「[接触して]上に」(⇔ off)

(13) The président said / that the matter was under
　　 大統領，社長　　　　　　　　　　　　　　　　考慮中
considerátion.

> - **under considerátion**（考慮中で）
> - **under constrúction**（建設中）
>   The bridge is under repair.（修理中）
>   The matter is under discússion.（討論中）

(14) This change means a depárture (from the traditional
　　　　　　　　　　　　　　　　　　出発→〜からの脱却　昔からの，伝統的な
way of condúcting eléctions.)
選挙を運営する方法

> - **departure from 〜**（〜からの脱却）
>   **departure for 〜**（〜へ向けての出発）

(15) The group criticized [批判した] the góvernment (for destróying the natural envíronment.)
（自然環境を破壊するという理由で政府を批判した）
〜という理由で
（早大・人間科学）

> 「賞罰の理由」を表す for
> - criticize A for B（BのことでAを批判する）
>   blame A for B（BのことでAを責める）
>   scold A for B（BのことでAを叱る）
>   reproach A for B（BのことでAを非難する）
>   punish A for B（BのことでAを罰する）
> - praise A for B（BのことでAをほめる）
>   admire A for B（BのことでAを賞賛する）
> - accuse A of B（BのことでAを責める，告訴する）
> - charge A with B（BのことでAを告発する）
>   accuse him of murder（殺人で告訴する）
>   charge him with stealing the money（窃盗で告発する）
>   ｝この２つは for ではない！

〔解答〕
(1) L (2) I (3) A (4) C (5) B (6) C (7) E (8) D
(9) K (10) F (11) G (12) H (13) J (14) D (15) C

TRACK 03

■ 群前置詞など　数語をまとめて１つの前置詞のように扱う

2 次の文の（　）に入れるのに適当な語句をア〜クから選びなさい。

(1) We went from Sendai to Aomori ((by way of) Morioka).
　　　　　　　　　　　　　　　　　　　　　盛岡を経由して

- **by way of ～ / via ～**（〜を経由して）

(2) The match was postpóned (on account of) a heavy rain.
　　　　　　　　　延期された　　　　　　〜のために（「理由」を表す）

- **because of ～ / on account of ～ / owing to ～**（〜のために）
- **thanks to ～**（〜のおかげで）

(3) Nagano will be connécted with Tokyo (by means of) a new expréssway.
　　　　　　　　　　　結ばれる　　　　　　　　　　　〜によって
　　　高速道路(motorway《英》)　　　　　　　　　　　　　　　　「手段」を表す

- **by means of ～**（〜［という手段］によって）
　　単数形も複数形も means

(4) [(In addition to) being pretty], Jane is very clever.
　　　〜に加えて　　　　　　　　(Jane is not only pretty but also very clever.)

- **in addition to ～ / besides ～ / on top of ～**（〜に加えて）
  - add A to B（A を B に加える）
  - add to ～（〜を増す）(increase)

248

(5) Taro <u>attended</u> the party (<u>for the purpose of</u>) seeing Junko there.
　　　　└〜に出席した　　　　　　〜する目的で

- **for the purpose of**
- **with a view to 〜ing**
  　　　　　　　　　　（〜する目的で）
  └動名詞 going, studying など
  　（go, study は×）

(6) [<u>As for</u> my baby], I'll <u>leave</u> her (<u>in the care of</u>) my mother.
　　└〜について言えば　　　　　　　in my mother's care
　　　　　　　　　　　　　　　　　　母の手に委ねよう

- **as for 〜**（〜について言えば）
  as to 〜（〜について）
- **leave ... in one's care / in the care of 〜**
  　　　　　　　　　　　　（…を〜の世話[管理]に委ねる）
  I left my pet in the care of a friend.（ペットを友だちに預けた）

- **according to 〜**（〜によると, 〜に応じて）
  according to ⎰ today's paper（今日の新聞によると）
  　　　　　　 ⎱ a recent survey（最近の調査によると）
  according to her instructions（彼女の指示に従って）

- **in comparison with 〜**（〜と比較して）
  My hometown is small in comparison with Tokyo.

ア. according to　　　　イ. for the purpose of
ウ. in addition to　　　　エ. in the care of
オ. on account of　　　　カ. by way of
キ. in comparison with　　ク. by means of

（小樽商大）

〔解答〕
(1) カ　(2) オ　(3) ク　(4) ウ　(5) イ　(6) エ

第18回　出題形式別・実戦問題演習(1)

TRACK 04

2文を対照して空所を埋める形式

《連立完成問題》

完全に同一ではない（文が変われば意味も多少は変わる）

3 次の各組の文がほぼ同じ意味を表すように，（　）の中に適当な1語を入れなさい。

(1) She <u>had a habit of</u> hitting the wrong key of the typewriter.

　　She (<u>would</u>) (<u>hit</u>) the wrong key of the typewriter.
　　　　　　　|　　　　　　　
　　　　　　[often]　habitually（習慣的に）を使うこともできるが…

> ● **would (often) ～ / used to ～**（よく～したものだ）

"my father = a most unhappy man"の状態で死んだ

(2) <u>My father</u> <u>died</u> <u>a most unhappy man</u>, [<u>although</u> he had
　　　S　　　　V　　　　　C　　　　　　ばく大な財産があったけれども
　　an imménse fórtune].

　　My father died a most unhappy man [(<u>for</u>) (<u>all</u>) his
　　　　　　　　　　　　　　　　　　　　　　　　　　|
　　immense fortune].　　　　　all ～を伴って「～にもかかわらず」

「あれだけばく大な財産がありながら（その割には）
死んだときはかなり不幸な人だった」

> ● **for all ～ / with all ～**（～にもかかわらず）
> 　　～の割には　　　　～をもってしても
> 　　～を考えると

251

(3) This is a plastic model of a ship (which I made myself). 自分で作った

This is a plastic model of a ship of (my) (own) making.

> ● of one's own ~ing（自分で〜した）
> a book of my own choosing / a book of my own choice など
> （私が自分で選んだ本）

(4) The house (whose roof is painted green) is my uncle's.

The house [the roof (of) (which) is painted green] is my uncle's.

> ● whose roof ...（← its roof） 所有格　もとの文を思い浮かべれば理解しやすい
> the roof of which ...（← the roof of the house ...）

(5) I advise you not to borrow money from your friends.
〜しないほうがいいと / 〜しないように　忠告する

You (had) (better) not borrow money from your friends.

I think you ought not to ...　否定語の位置に注意

> ● had better 〜（〜するほうがいい，〜しなさい）
> had better not 〜（〜ないほうがいい）　やや命令的
> should 〜 / ought to 〜（〜すべきだ）
> ● it is advisable for ... to 〜（〜するのが賢明だ）
> it would be better for ... to 〜（…は〜するほうがいいだろう）

- ... **might as well** ~ (~してもよろしいのでは)
  You might as well go (as stay home).

(6) I am sorry / that she is absent from the conference.
   欠席している[形容詞]　　　　　　　会議

   I am sorry / about (her) (ábsence) from the conference.
   残念に思う　　　　　　欠席すること[名詞]

- be absent from ~ (~を欠席している) (⇔ be present at ~)
- one's absence from ~ (…の~からの欠席
   →…が~を欠席していること)

  I'm sorry (that) ... ── that ... は節（口語的）
  I'm sorry about ~ ── about ~ は句（文語的）
    └ "前置詞＋名詞"を多用している
       句の多い文は文語的になる

彼があんなに強いとは思わなかった
(7) I didn't expect him to be so strong.
      V   O   C

   He is (stronger) (than) I expected.
              予想以上に強い

- **not so ... (as ~)** → 比較級 than ~ (~ほど…でない → ~より…)

(8) Would you <u>mind</u> my moving your car ? 　　　かまう，気にする

Would you [<u>objéct</u> [(if) I (<u>moved</u>) your car]?
　　　　　　 mind — 異議がある，反対する

> - **mind ～ing**（～するのを気にする）
> - **Do you mind if ...?**　　— if I <u>move</u> your car?　) if ... を用いるのが
>   **Would you mind if ...?**　— if I <u>moved</u> your car?　) 口語的
>   （～してもかまいませんか，～してよろしいでしょうか）

(9) They planned to cross the river / but failed.

They planned to cross the river (<u>only</u>) (<u>to</u>) fail.
　　　　　　　　　　　　　　　　　　⇒　「結果」を表す不定詞の１つ

渡ろうと計画したが失敗した

> - **only to fail / in vain / without success**（[…したが]結局はだめだった）

(10) His brother had <u>a fatal wound</u> (<u>in the chest</u>) yesterday.
　　　　　　　　　　致命的な負傷　　　胸部に

His brother was (<u>fatally</u>)(<u>wounded</u>) in the chest yesterday.
　　　　　　　　　　　　　　　　　　breastは「（女性の）乳房」　（小樽商大）

> - **fatal**（致命的な）〈形容詞〉
>   **fatally**（致命的に）〈副詞〉
> - **be injured / get injured**（[一般的に]けがをする）
>   **be hurt / get hurt**（[比較的軽い]けがをする）
>   **be wounded / get wounded**（負傷する）

〔解答〕
(1) would hit / habitually hit   (2) for all / with all   (3) my own
(4) of which   (5) had better   (6) her absence
(7) stronger than   (8) if, moved   (9) only to
(10) fatally wounded

《書き出し指定完成問題》

4 次の日本文に相当する意味になるように空所を埋め，英文を完成させなさい。

(1) 彼は(映画を見ている間に)時計を修繕してもらった。

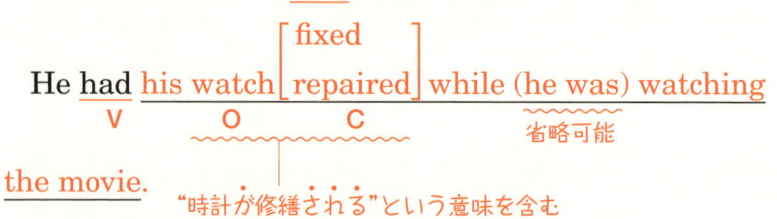

　　　　　　　　　　　　　　　while ...

He had his watch [fixed / repaired] while (he was) watching the movie.
　V　　　O　　　　　C　　　　　　　　省略可能

"時計が修繕される"という意味を含む

- while ... （…する間に）
- have + O + p.p. （[…が〜されるように]してもらう[させる]）

(2) (彼女が帰るまで)待つよりほかに仕方がないと思った。

I thought that [I would have to wait till[until] she came back.
　　　　　　　　I could do nothing but wait ...

- till ... / until ... （…するまで）
- will have to 〜 （〜しなければならないだろう）
- can do nothing but 〜 （〜するよりしかたない）　原形不定詞
- there is nothing for it but to 〜 （〜するよりほかない）
- have no choice but to 〜 （〜するよりほか[の選択は]ない）

第18回　出題形式別・実戦問題演習(1)

(3)　(10分ほど歩くと)(子供のころによく泳いだ)川に出た。
After I walked about ten minutes, I came to the river (where ...).

⇨ About ten minutes' walk brought me to the river

$\begin{bmatrix} \text{where} \\ \text{in which} \end{bmatrix}$ I would often swim $\begin{bmatrix} \text{when (I was) a child.} \\ \text{in my childhood.} \end{bmatrix}$

- bring － brought － brought(～を連れてくる)
- I used to swim there → where ...　　副詞だから関係副詞 where
  I would often swim in the river → in which …

(4)　私たちは健康に有害な食品を(知らずに)食べていることがよくある。
　　harmful to our health　　　before we know it / without knowing it

We often eat $\begin{bmatrix} \text{food [which} \\ \text{(that)} \\ \text{such food as} \end{bmatrix}$ is harmful to our health]

without knowing it.

（関西学院大・文）

- ... which ～　　　｝（～のような…）
  such ... as ～
  └ 先行詞に such がつくと関係代名詞は as
- before one knows it / without knowing it / unconsciously
  （知らないうちに，無意識で）

〔解答〕
(1) He had his watch repaired while (he was) watching the movie.
(2) I thought that there was nothing for it but to wait till she came back.
(3) About ten minutes' walk brought me to the river in which I used to swim when I was a child.
(4) We often eat food (which is) harmful to our health without knowing it.

第 19 回

出題形式別・実戦問題演習 (2)

[以前は誤文訂正(「誤りあらば直せ(Correct errors, if any.)」)
現在は誤り箇所の選択問題が非常に多い。形式にも慣れておくこと]

《正誤判定問題》

1 次の英文のA～Dのうち，誤った英語を含んだ部分がある場合にはA～Dの中の1つを，誤りがない場合にはEを選びなさい。

(1) [After ᴬworking with the company (for ᴮover 40 years)], he ᶜwas elected as ᴰpresident. ᴱNO ERROR

　会社で働く / 40年以上 / 選ばれた / 社長
　無冠詞（身分，公職など）

- **president**（大統領, 社長）
  mayor（市長）, **governor**（知事）, **captain**（長, 船長, 主将）
  chairman, chairperson（議長）

　これらは文の補語(C)では冠詞をつけない

(2) The old couple ᴬare ᴮconsidering ᶜof living in a cottage (ᴰseparated from the neighbors). ᴱNO ERROR

　老夫婦 / 不要！ / 小屋・別荘 / 切り離された
　単数形だが複数扱い

- **consider ～ing / be thinking of ～ing**（～することを考える）

(3) We ᴬwill be ᴮsure to visit you again [ᶜwhen ᴰyou are convenient]. ᴱNO ERROR

きっと訪ねるだろう（sure to visit）
(×) when you are convenient → it is (○)

- when you are convénient（×）人間を主語にしない！
- when it is convenient (for you)（○）

(4) ᴬNot ᴮall of Japanése can recognize ᶜevery cháracter (ᴰused to print Japanese newspapers). ᴱNO ERROR

トル！（of を取る）
漢字（character）
～に使われる（used to print）

- all the Japanese（○）
- all of Japanese（×）
- all of the Japanese（○）

- **all ~s / all of the ~s**
    all students / all of the students
- **most ~s / most of the ~s**（大部分の～，～の大部分）
    most students / most of the students　これらが自然な形
- **not all ~**（すべての～が…だとは限らない）〈部分否定〉

(5) I ᴬhave been dreaming [ᴮto climb the mountain (to watch the sun ᶜrise above ᴰthe horizon)]. ᴱNO ERROR

of climbing（○）
× to climb
V′ (to watch)
O′ (the sun)　C′ (rise)
原形不定詞（○）
水平線（the horizon）

- **dream of ~ing**（～するのを夢想する，夢に描く）

(6) A ᴬlarge group of people [ᴮwas gathering [around the
   　　○　　　　　　　　　　　　[were(○)
   大勢の人たち(複数扱い)　　　　　×　　　　ベンチで眠る少女のまわりに

little girl (ᶜsleeping ᴰon the bench)]. ᴱNO ERROR

- a large group of ～ / a large number of ～（大勢の～）→複数扱い

TRACK 02

(7) ᴬA quite remarkable interest (in ᴮdinosaurs) ᶜhave been
   　　　著しい　　　興味　　　　恐竜　　　has(○)
   　　　　　　　　　　　　　　　　　　　　　　×
   　　　　　　　　　　 S　　　　　　　　　　　V

developing [among people (ᴰgoing to movie theaters)].
ᴱNO ERROR

- 主語(S)と動詞(V)の数の一致
  └頻出！

(8) ᴬAnyone (ᴮinterested) is eligible for the contest
   　　　　　　　　　　　～の資格がある　コンテスト，競技会

[ᶜregardless of ᴰage, sex and nationality]. ᴱNO ERROR
   ～にかかわらず　　　　　×
   (whether ... or ～)　or(○)
   　　　　　　　　「年齢，性別，国籍のいかんにかかわらず」

- regardless of A, B or C（A，B，Cのいかんにかかわらず）

第19回　出題形式別・実戦問題演習(2)

(9) The storm ᴬis bringing ᴮhigh winds and rain / ᶜbut causing no ᴰmajor damages(×). ᴱNO ERROR

　大きな災害　　　U｜C だが通例 U　cause heavy damage（大災害を引き起こす）

- **cause damage (to ...) / do damage (to ...)**（…に損害を与える）

(10) ᴬThe dark clouds suggested（それとなく示していた） / that ᴮthe weather ᶜdid not(×) improve since ᴰyesterday. ᴱNO ERROR

　　　　had not improved(○)（よくなっていない）
　　この語に注目！
　　「今朝起きてみたら昨日から…だった」と考えると yesterday はこのまま OK

昨日から[過去の1時点以来] → 完了形を使う
「黒い雲が…を示していた」→「黒い雲を見ると…だとわかった」

- 現在完了 ... since ～
- 過去完了 ... since ～　　}（～[して]以来, …）

(11) Japanese people invite ᴬoutsiders（外部の人たちを） ᴮinto their homes（「招き入れる」という感じ(○)） [ᶜmuch less often (than ᴰthe British does(×))]. ᴱNO ERROR

　比較級の強めは much(○)　　複数扱い　do(○)

- **the Japanese / (the) Japanese people**（日本人）
  the Japanese people（日本国民）
  ↑やや文語的
- **the British / (the) British people**（イギリス人，英国人）

　　　　　　　　　　　　　　　　　　　　　　複数扱い

263

(12) "How many ᴬcopies do you want to ᴮhave printed?" (◎)

"ᶜFive hundred, I ᴰwould say." ᴱNO ERROR

（早大・人間科学）

「何部コピーをとってもらいたい？」「500部というところでしょうか」

- have copies printed → How many copies ...?
  V   O   C
  └ I want to have ten copies printed. (◎)
  （10枚コピーをとってもらいたい）

〔解答〕
(1) E　(2) C　(3) D　(4) B　(5) B　(6) B
(7) C　(8) D　(9) D　(10) C　(11) D　(12) E

第19回　出題形式別・実戦問題演習(2)

TRACK 03

誤りの箇所を指摘させる問題は頻出形式の1つ
（TOEFL，TOEICでも出題されている）

《誤文訂正問題》

2 次の各英文の下線部A〜Dの中に，文法的，あるいは，語法的な誤りが1つずつある。その箇所を指摘し，正しい英語に直しなさい。

(1) Ken changed his májor（専攻科目） ᴬfrom French to English, / ᴮhoping ᶜto find a job ᴰmore easy.
　　　　　　　　　　　　　　　　　　　　×
　　仕事をもっとたやすく　　　○ easily（副詞）　　find a job easy
　　見つけられるようにと　　　　　　　　　　　　（仕事がやさしいとわかる）
　　　　　　　　　　　　　　　　　　　　　　　　と区別！

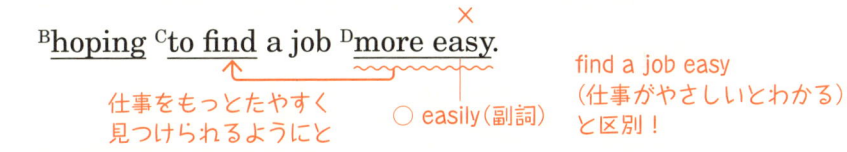

- easy — easier — easiest 〈形容詞〉
  easily — more easily — most easily 〈副詞〉
- major in（〜を専攻する）
  What's your major? / What do you major in?（何をご専攻ですか）
  one's major（…の専攻科目）

(2) I ᴬtalked with the president（社長，大統領）(every night) (ᴮfor two months) / and ᶜfound it ᴰexhausted.
　　　　　　　　　　　　　　　　　　　　　　　　　　　　V　O　　C　　○ exhausting
　　それが私を疲れさせることがわかった

- exhausting（［人を］疲れさせる）　It's exhausting.　　区別！
  exhausted（［人が］疲れて）　　　I'm exhausted.
- find + O + C の "O + C" に注目

(3) ᴬThere was ᴮa striking resémblance (ᶜamong ᴰthe mother and baby).

　　　　　　　　　　　○ between（母と子の[2人の]間に）
　　　　　　難しい類似　　　×（3つ以上の）それらの間

- **between A and B**（AとBの間で）
  among ～s（[3つ以上の] ～の間で）

(4) (ᴬFrom the móment I saw her), ᴮI knew / ᶜthat she was ᴰa really politícian.
　　　　　　　　　　　　　　　　　　　　　× / ○ real　本当の政治家（政治屋）

- **real**（本当の）〈形容詞〉
  really（本当に，まったく）〈副詞〉
  She's a real politician. ｝区別！
  She's really a politician.

　　　　　　　歩いていると気づいた（「気づいたとき歩いていた」は△×）
　　　　　　　　　　　　　　　⇨　　　　○ realized
(5) I ᴬwas walking along the street / when I ᴮwas réalizing that a detéctive, (whom I ᶜhad seen twice already that day), ᴰwas following me.
　　　　　　　探偵
　　　　私の後をつけていた

- **be ～ing**〈進行形〉... **when** ......
  （～していると[するとそのとき] …）

第19回 出題形式別・実戦問題演習(2)

- had p.p.〈過去完了〉... when ......
  ⇒
  (〜してしまうと[するとそのとき] …)
  I was going to reply when John cut in.
  (私が答えようとすると，そこへジョンが口をはさんだ)
  I had fallen asleep when someone knocked at the door.
  (私が眠りにつくとだれかがドアをノックした)

TRACK 04

(6) The deluxe tour ᴬof Andes includes ᴮa two-day stay (at ᶜthe spectacular Machu Pichu ᴰruins).

豪華な旅　○ the　　　　〜を含む　　　単数形でよい(○)
　　　　　　　　　　　　　　　　　　 a two days' stay (○)
壮観な　　　　　　　　 廃墟，遺跡　　(2日間の滞在)

- 固有名詞と定冠詞
  the Andes（アンデス山脈）/ the Alps（アルプス山脈）
  the Rocky Mountains（ロッキー山脈）
  　複数形の固有名詞に the がつく！
  　the United States
  　the Obamas（オバマ一家）
- a two-day stay / a two days' stay（2日間の滞在）
  a three-year-old boy（3歳の男の子）
  　　　　　　　　　　　　　　　　　— day's は×（注意！）
  　単数形でよい

(7) [ᴬAs there will be an agent (at the airport) (ᴮto meet you) (as soon as you ᶜarrived in New York)], you ᴰneedn't worry about changing money or reserving a hotel.

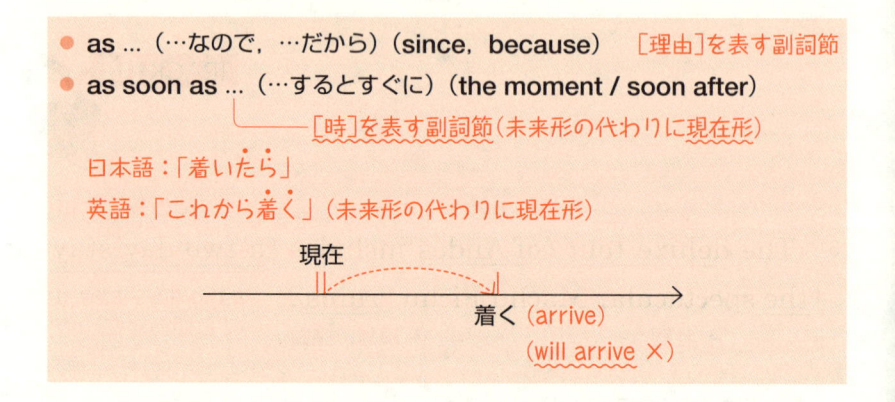

- **as ...** (…なので，…だから) (since, because) ［理由］を表す副詞節
- **as soon as ...** (…するとすぐに) (the moment / soon after) ［時］を表す副詞節（未来形の代わりに現在形）

日本語：「着いたら」
英語：「これから着く」（未来形の代わりに現在形）

現在 → 着く (arrive) (will arrive ×)

(8) Tom's decayed teeth ᴬwere troubling him, / so he went to a dental surgeon (ᴮto see about having ᶜthem ᴰpull).

I'll see about that.
(考えておきましょう)

("虫歯が抜かれる"という関係)

- **have + O + 原形不定詞**（[…が〜するように] させる，してもらう）
  "…が〜する"（能動）の関係を含む
- **have + O + p.p.**（[…が〜されるように] してもらう，させる）
  "…が〜される"（受動）の関係を含む

  I had a dental surgeon pull my teeth. (○)
  I had my teeth pulled (by a dental surgeon). (○)

(9) The witness reported / that he ᴬsaw the suspect ᴮleft the bank ᶜ(carrying a flight bag and ᴰarmed with a gun).

　　had seen も可
　　証人　〜と伝えた　　　　容疑者　×
　　飛行用バッグ　　銃で武装して
　　「…容疑者が銀行を出て行くのを見たと」
　　leave (○)
　　leaving (○)

- **see + O + 原形不定詞**（…が〜するのを見る）
  see + O + 〜ing（…が〜しているのを見る）

(10) ᴬ[The harder I tried ᴮto convince him ᶜto change his mind], the more ᴰdetermination he was to carry out the project.　　　　　　　　　　　　　　　　　　　　（長崎大）

　　　　　　　　　　…に〜するように説得する
　　　　　　　　　　×
　　　　　　　　　　○ determined
　　　　　　　　　　実行する
　　その分だけますます〜
　　計画

「私が（彼に）心を変えるよう説得しようとすればするほど，彼は計画を実行する決意を（それだけ）ますます固めた」

- **The 比較級 ..., the 比較級 ～**（…すればするほどますます～）
  I tried hard to ～ → The harder I tried to ～
  He was determined to ～ → the more determined he was to ～
- **convince ... to ～**（…に～するように説得する）(persuade ... to ～)
  convince A of B（A に B を納得させる）
- **be determined to ～**（～しようと決意する）

〔解答〕
(1) D → more easily　　(2) D → exhausting　　(3) C → between
(4) D → a real politician　　(5) B → realized
(6) A → of the Andes　　(7) C → arrive　　(8) D → pulled
(9) B → leaving / leave　　(10) D → determined

《誤文選択問題》

3 次の各組の英文より，文法的，語法的に誤っているものをそれぞれ1つ選びなさい。

(1) イ．The school <u>awarded</u> <u>Mary</u> <u>a prize</u> <u>for</u> her good work.
　　　　　　　　V　　　 O′　　O

　　ロ．I suppose / <u>I</u> <u>felt</u> slightly <u>jéalous</u>. （I ＝ jealous）（jealously は×）
　　　　　　　　　　S′ V′　　　　　　　C′
　　　　　　　　　　　　　嫉妬している，ねたんでいる

　　ハ．His áttitude suggests / that he is <u>not really</u>
　　　　　　　態度　　　　　　　　　　　あまり興味がない
　　　interested.

　　ニ．I <u>apólogized</u> <u>for him</u> <u>to have</u> stepped on his foot.
　　　　　　　　　　　　○ to him　 for having
　　　　足を踏んだことを彼に謝った

● award ＋ O′ ＋ O（…に〜を授ける）
　award A for B（BのことでAを授ける）
　　　　　　[賞罰の理由]を表す
● feel ＋ C（〜だと感じる）
● not really 〜（あまり〜でない）
● apologize (to) A (for) B（AにBのことを謝る）
　excuse A for B（AにBのことを謝る／言い訳をする）
　thank A for B（AにBの礼を言う）

(2) イ．She was pressing her nose against the window.
〇 窓に鼻を押しつける

ロ．You should not talk about Jack behind his back.
〇 〜のいない所で

ハ．My mother asked me to go for errand.
× 使いに行く（〇 go on an errand）

ニ．We are very much obliged to you for your help.
本当にありがとう存じます

■ **慣用的な前置詞**
- **press ... against** 〜（〜に…を押しつける）
  lean against the wall（壁によりかかる）
- **behind** one's back（〜のいない所で）
  in one's face（〜の目の前で）
  to one's face（〜に面と向かって）
- **go on an errand / go on errands**（使いに行く）
  go on a trip / go on a journey（旅行に行く）
- **go for a walk**（散歩に行く）
  go for a swim / go swimming（泳ぎに行く）
  go shopping（買い物に行く）
- **be obliged to A for B**（A に対して B のことをありがたく思っている）

(3) イ．There were beads of sweat (on his forehead).

　ロ．He gave me lots of valuable advices (on my study of biology).

　ハ．Cats belong to one class of animals, / while fish to another.

　ニ．This store carries a wide range of household equipment.

> ● 複数形にしない名詞
> 　advice(忠告)，information(情報)，machinery(機械装置)，
> 　furniture(家具類)，equipment(備品，機器)，homework(宿題)，
> 　luggage / baggage(荷物)
> 　数えるときは a piece of ～，two pieces of ～など
> ● belong to ～（～に属する）
> 　　進行形にしない動詞

(4) イ．He had no company (on the journey).

　ロ．The expression (on his face) betrayed his feelings.

　ハ．The hospital has to accept emergency cases (resulting from) natural disasters.

　ニ．He came here / on the purpose for borrowing some money from me.　　for the purpose of (～する目的で)

- **cómpany**（仲間 ← 〜と一緒にいること）
  I don't like my father's company.
      父の会社 / 父と一緒にいること
- **result from 〜**（〜から生じる）
  result in 〜（〜という結果になる）
- **for the purpose of 〜ing**
  with the view of 〜ing / with a view to 〜ing （〜する目的で）
  　　　　　　　　　　　　　　　　　　動名詞！

(5) イ．Will three o'clock be convénient for you? [all right with you?]

ロ．Most people were favorite to the idéa. ×
　　　　　　　　　　　[for 〜 / in favor of 〜]
　　　　　　　　　　　（〜に賛成である）

ハ．I'm always suspícious of men like him.
　　　　　　　　　　　〜を疑わしいと思う

ニ．Four lívely youngsters suddenly burst (into the room). [láivli]（発音に注意）　　空き部屋に入ってきた
　　　　　　　　元気のいい，陽気な

- **be convénient for 〜 / be all right with 〜**（〜に都合がいい）
- **in favor of 〜 / for 〜**（〜に賛成である）
- **be suspícious of 〜**（〜を疑っている）← suspéct（疑う）

(6) イ． The mayor (to whom she wrote a letter) told her the truth.

ロ．He was accused for a crime of violence (which he was innocent.)
　　　　　　　×→of　　　　　　　　　　×／of which ... / which ... of
　　　　　　　　　　　　　　　　　　　　　　　　　of

ハ．I have no intention whatever of resigning.
　　　　　　　　　　　　否定の強め
　　　　　　辞職する考えは毛頭ない

ニ．What he really needs is a nice cup of tea.
　　　　　S　　　　　　　V　　C

（関西学院大・理）

- accuse A of B（AをBのことで告訴する）
  A is accused of B（AはBのことで告訴されている）
- be innocent of ～（～について罪がない，潔白である）
  be guilty of ～（～について罪がある）
- no ... whatever / not ... at all（全く…でない）
  　否定語を強める
- not ... in the least（少しも…でない）

〔解答〕
(1) ニ　(2) ハ　(3) ロ　(4) ニ　(5) ロ　(6) ロ

第 20 回

出題形式別・実戦問題演習 (3)

TRACK 01

《整序問題》 ── 語句の並べ換えには文法と語句の知識が必要
手がかり(clue)となる構文・語句がひらめくかどうか

1 次の日本文の意味を表すように, ( )中の語句を並べ換えて英文を完成させなさい。

(1) あの歌を聞くと必ず高校時代を思い出す。 →「思い出さずには聞けない」という発想

I (that / hear / never / remembering / song / without) my high school days. ── 二重否定 ──

I never hear that song without remembering my high school days.

これらも既出 ─ thinking of ～ / being reminded of ～

- never ... without ～ing / cannot ... without ～ing
　　　　　　　　　　　　　　　　　(…すれば必ず～する)
- remember ～ / be reminded of ～ （～を思い出す）
　　　　　　← remind A of B （A に B を思い出させる）

(2) この帽子を見て何を思い出しますか。 →「この帽子があなたに何を思い出させるか」という発想

What (of / remind / this / hat / you / does)?

What does this hat remind you of?

〈参考〉What are you reminded of by this hat?

- remind A of B （A に B を思い出させる）
　A is reminded of B （A は B を思い出す）

(3) 話し出してから，初めて彼だとわかった。 → not until ...

It was not (speak / heard / I / him / that / until) I recognized him.

It was not until I heard him speak that I recognized him.
　　　　　　　　　　　V′　O′　C′（原形不定詞）

- not ... until ～（～するまで…でない）
  → It is not until ～ that ...（～してはじめて…する）
  　　　　ここを強める強調構文
- hear ＋ O ＋ 原形不定詞（…が～するのを聞く）

(4) 彼女のことを考えまいとしても無理だった。 → It(S) ... for ... to ～の形式

It (impossible / was / not / me / to / for) think of her.

It was impossible for me not to think of her.
　　　　　　　　　　　　　　この位置にも注意　　((1) - (4) 関西学院大・経)

- It is impossible for ... to ～（…が～するのは不可能だ）
- not to ～ — not(否定語)は不定詞の直前に！

TRACK 02

(5) (先日貸した) 本を返してもらいたい。 → want you to ～

I (I / lent you / return / the book / to / want / you) the other day. ─ want to ～（私が～したい）は×

I want you to return the book (I lent you the other day).

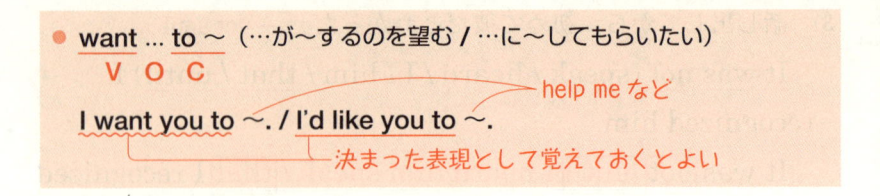

> - **want ... to ~** (…が～するのを望む / …に～してもらいたい)
>   V O C
>   **I want you to ~. / I'd like you to ~.**
>   （help me など / 決まった表現として覚えておくとよい）

(6) (明日の今頃は) 汽車の旅に出かけていることでしょう。→ 未来進行形

　　At (be traveling / on / the train / this / time / tomorrow / we will).

　　(At this time tomorrow) we will be traveling on the train.

> - **(at) this time tomorrow / now tomorrow** （明日の今頃）
>   「来年の今頃」なら **about this time next year**
> - **will be ~ing**
>   Our train will be arriving at Tokyo soon.
>   （列車はまもなく東京駅へ到着します）

(7) ちょっとそれを開けてくれませんか。→ be kind enough to ~

　　Perhaps (be / enough / it / kind / open / to / would / you).

　　Perhaps you would be kind enough to open it.
　　（ご親切に～してくださいますね）

> - **Would you kindly ...? / Could you kindly ...?** ┐
>   **Would you be kind enough to ~?**   ├ 丁寧な依頼
>   　→ Perhaps you would be kind enough to ~.   ┘

(8) 行きたくなくても行かねばなりません。 → whether ... or not

You've (go / got / it / like / or / to / whether / you) not.

You've got to go / whether you like it or not.
　　　　　　　　　　　　好むと好まざるとにかかわらず　　((5)-(8)早大・法)

> ● must ～ / have to ～ / have got to ～（～しなければならない）
> 　I've got to ～.　　　　｝などと口ずさんで覚える
> 　You've got to ～.　　　（くだけると you got to ～も）
> ● whether ... or not（…であろうとなかろうと）

〔解答〕
(1) I never hear that song without remembering my high school days.
(2) What does this hat remind you of?
(3) It was not until I heard him speak that I recognized him.
(4) It was impossible for me not to think of her.
(5) I want you to return the book I lent you the other day.
(6) At this time tomorrow we will be traveling on the train.
(7) Perhaps you would be kind enough to open it.
(8) You've got to go whether you like it or not.

《選択整序問題》

2 英文の空所すべてに，それぞれの下に与えられた語の中から最も適当な1語を選んで入れ，日本文の意味になるようにしなさい。選択肢は3語ずつ余分に与えてある。使用は1語1回かぎりとする。

―指示を見落とさないように！

viewpoints
物の見方，視点

(1) 新しい見地が伝統的な見地にとって代わった。

Traditional (víewpoints) (gave) (place) (to) (newer) (ones).

「場所をゆずった」という感じ

(イ) gave　　×(ロ) had　　(ハ) newer
(ニ) ones　　(ホ) place　　×(ヘ) sùbstituted

substitute ... for ～（～の代わりに…を用いる）

×(ト) took　　(チ) to　　(リ) víewpoints

B takes place of A（B が A に代わる）

- A → B（A に代わって B になる）
  A gives place to B.
  B takes the place of A. / A is taken the place of by B.

  ―take the place of の受動態

  B replaces A. / A is replaced by B.

  （A が B に取って代わられる）

- sùbstitute B for A（A の代わりに B を代用する）

(2) あの小道は（雨が降ると）ぬかるみやすい。 → be apt for ～

That (path) (is) (apt) (to) (be) (muddy) (after) (rain).

(イ) after　×(ロ) always　(ハ) apt　(ニ) be　×(ホ) easily
(ヘ) is　(ト) muddy　(チ) path　(リ) rain　×(ヌ) seldom（めったに～しない）
(ル) to

- be easy to get muddy ／ easily get muddy （ぬかるみやすい）
- be apt to ～（～する傾向がある，～しがちだ）

(3) 君は英語で用が足せますか？　（自分の意思を相手にわかってもらえますか）

Can (you) (make) (yourself) (understood) (in) (English)?

(イ) English　(ロ) in　×(ハ) let　(ニ) make
×(ホ) to　×(ヘ) understand　○(ト) understood　←ここがポイント
(チ) you　(リ) yourself

- make + O + p.p.（…が～されるようにする）
- make oneself understood
    　　（「自分の意志が(相手に)理解される」ようにする）
- get one's meaning across（意味を通じさせる）
- commúnicate (with each other)（お互いに意思を通じ合う）

(4) 彼はそれを１人ですることを何とも思っていない。
　　　　　　　do it by himself
　　　　　　　　　　　　　　　　　think nothing of ～

He (thinks) (nothing) (of) (doing) (it) (by) (himself).
　　　　　　　　　　　　　　　　　　　　　　　　　　　by himself

(イ) by　　　×(ロ) does　　(ハ) doing　　(ニ) himself
(ホ) it　　　×(ヘ) not　　 (ト) nothing　(チ) of
×(リ) think　(ヌ) thinks

(学習院大・文)

- by oneself（ひとりで）(alone)
- think much of ～ / think highly of ～（～を重んじる）
  think nothing of ～ / think little of ～（～を何とも思わない）
- make much of ～（～を尊重する）
  make nothing of ～ / make little of ～（～を軽んじる）

〔解答〕
(1) (リ)(イ)(ホ)(チ)(ハ)(ニ)　(2) (チ)(ヘ)(ハ)(ル)(ニ)(ト)(イ)(リ)
(3) (チ)(ニ)(リ)(ト)(ロ)(イ)　(4) (ヌ)(ト)(チ)(ハ)(ホ)(イ)(ニ)

第 20 回　出題形式別・実戦問題演習(3)

TRACK 04

《語数指定英訳問題》　→"条件つき"の英作文(文法問題に近い)

3　それぞれ指定の語数で英語に訳しなさい。[　]の中に与えられた語句をそのままの順序で，形を変えずに用いること。don't などの短縮形は 1 語に数え，コンマ，ピリオド，疑問符などは 1 語に数えない。

(1) この湖の深さはどのくらいだと思いますか。(8 語)
[think / is]
　　　　　　　　　　　　── do you think の位置は？

How deep do you think this lake is?
　　　　　V　S　　　　　　S´　V´

- 疑問詞 + V + S?　　　｝1 文にすると？
  Do you think …?　　→ 疑問詞 do you think S´ V´ ?
  　　　　　　　　　　　　　　　　　　　　ここの語順にも
  　　　　　　　　　　　　　　　　　　　　注意する！

- How deep is S? + do you think
  → How deep do you think + S + is?
  　　　疑問文の語順　　S´ V´ の語順
  What is the depth of ～? + do you think
  → What do you think the depth of ～ is?
  　　　　　　　　　　　S´　　　　　　V´

(2) 私はそれが誰のものか知りたい。(8語)
　　[I'd / belongs]　└─belong to 〜を使う

I'd like to know / who it belongs to.
　　　　　　　　　　[whom it belongs to.　] これらも文法的
　　　　　　　　　　[to whom it belongs.　] には OK

- **I'd like to 〜**（〜したいのですが）
- **belong to 〜**（〜に属する，〜のものだ）

　　　　since / since then / since that time
　　　　　　　　┌─often / many times / a lot of times
(3) あれから 何回も お手紙を差し上げました。(8語か9語)
　　[written / times]　└─write (to) 〜

I have written (to) you many times [a lot of times] since then.　（since とともに現在完了）

- **have + p.p. ... since 〜**（〜以来…した / している）
- **since / since then / since that time**（あのとき以来）
- **often / many times / a lot of times / lots of times**（何度も）
- **write to 〜 / write (to) 〜 / write a letter to 〜**（〜に手紙を書く）

(4) 彼女は(子供を助けようとして)もう少しでおぼれるところだった。
　　　　　　　　　　　trying to rescue the child(5語)→残り3, 4語
[drowned /rescue]　　　　　　　　　　　　　　　　（8語か9語）

She ⎡ was almost drowned　　　　⎤ trying to rescue the child.
　　 ⎢ nearly drowned　　　　　　 ⎥
　　 ⎣ [came near being drowned] ⎦
　　　　　└─ 語数が合わない

- **almost / nearly / come near 〜ing**（もう少しで〜するところ）
  barely（かろうじて，なんとか）
  　She barely escaped drowning.（危うくおぼれないですんだ）
- **drown / be drowned / get drowned**（おぼれる）
  　└─ 自動詞でも他動詞でも使う

(5) 今決定するにはまだ早すぎる。（9語）　→ too ... to 〜
　　　　decide → make a decision
[far / early / make / now]
　too 〜を強める副詞

It's far too early to make a decision now.
[← It is]

- **decide / make a decision**（決める，決定する）
- **(far) too ... to 〜**（〜するにはあまりにも…すぎる，あまりにも…で〜できない）

(6) 彼は会議で自分の考えをわかってもらうのに苦労した。(**11**語)
　　　　　　　　　　　↑
　　　　　　make oneself understood

[hard time / himself / at the meeting]

He had a hard time making himself understood at the meeting.
　　　　　　　　　　　　　　　　　　(× understand)

（早大・法）

> - **make oneself understood**（自分の考えが［相手に］理解されるようにする）
> - have a hard time ～ing ⎫
> - have trouble (in) ～ing ⎬ （～するのに苦労する）
> - have difficulty (in) ～ing ⎭
>
> She had a hard time finding her hotel.
> （ホテルがなかなか見つからなかった）

〔解答〕
(1) How deep do you think this lake is?
(2) I'd like to know who it belongs to.
(3) I've written to you many times since then.
　　I've written you a lot of times since then.
(4) She nearly drowned trying to rescue the child.
　　She was almost drowned trying to rescue the child.
(5) It's far too early to make a decision now.
(6) He had a hard time making himself understood at the meeting.

第20回　出題形式別・実戦問題演習(3)

TRACK 06

■ 英文の特徴 ── 日本語と異なる点を5項目(大きく心得ておくとよい)

① "S + V + X + X" という基本構造　　（日本語はばく然と
　　└ 英語はこの形をとる！　　　　　　　状況を述べる）

② S + V + O + X ── 英語は「主語(S)が〜を(O)…する(V)」
　 S + V + O + C　など　　という組み立てをする。
　　　└ この理解は大事！　　（例）「写真が私に〜を思い出させる／
　　　　　　　　　　　　　　　　このバスが私を〜へ連れて行く」など

③ 「名詞」中心の文構成　　（日本語は「動詞」中心の表現）

　　　"N of N" など ── 「前置詞と名詞」の組み合わせが多い！◎

　　（例）the parent's love of their daughter など
　　　　（両親が娘をかわいがること）
　　　　A moment's thought will make it clear. [英語]　┐比較！
　　　　（ちょっと考えればわかるよ）　　　　　[日本語] ┘

④ 「後置修飾」の構造　　（日本語は前から修飾する）
　　　　　　　　　　　　英語は後ろから修飾することが多い！

　　　　⎡ prep. + N　　　　　　⎤
　　　　⎢ to 不定詞　　　　　　⎥　名詞を中心に文を構成するので
　　 N ⎢ 〜ing/ p.p. ...　　　⎥　こういう形がきわめて多い ◎
　　　　⎣ 関係詞 ... など　　　⎦

⑤ 副詞的要素
　　　S + V + more **Adj.** [than S' + V' + X' + X'] など
　　　　　　　　　　　　　　　　└ 副詞節

骨組みのS + V + Cなどの形容詞や副詞に副詞句・副詞節などが修飾する
形も多い。→何が何を修飾するのかをつかまないといけない
◎

以上で英文法(英語の形からの理解)は終了です。ここまでよくついてきてくれました。必ずその努力は稔ります。かなりの力と自信がついたでしょう。さらに英語力を充実させるのに必要なのは，内容的に興味のある文を大量に読むことだけです。

　大学入試はもちろん，その後も広い場所で自由に英語力を伸ばしますように。成功を祈ります♡♡

索引

*文型・文法事項・重要語句などをアルファベット順に示しています。
*日本語の用語は，ローマ字に直して検索してください。

《注》ジ，ジャ，ジュ，ジョ → ji, ja, ju, jo
シ，シャ，シュ，ショ → shi, sha, shu, sho
チ，チャ，チュ，チョ → chi, cha, chu, cho
ツ → tsu；フ → fu

A

a / an ＋固有名詞	121
A and B	83
a black and white cat	82
a black cat and a white one	82
a chair to sit on	94
A excels B.	166
a good[great] deal of	95, 144
a good way	95
A is one thing and B is another.	125
A is preferable to B.	166
A is reminded of B.	15, 21, 278
A is robbed of B.	42
a large group of ～	262
a large number of ～	143, 262
a lot of ～	143
a man of ～	131
a number of ～	83
A or B	82
a piece of ～	116, 273
a poet and novelist	82
A to B	228
A (together) with B	83
able と possible	138
according to ～	249
accuse A of B	247, 275
add A to B	248
add to ～	248
admire A for B	247
admit ～ing	104, 106
advice	116, 273
after ...	218
against ～	113, 227, 232, 243
all of which ...	158
all ～s / all of the ～s	261
(all) the 比較級 ... because ...	171
(all) the 比較級 for ～	171
all the more ...	171
almost / nearly と barely	287
also	136
also, too と not ... either	135-136
although ...	251
always ... not	199
among ～s	266
... and ...	208
..., and so ...	215
another	125
answer	13
anything but ～	192
apologize to A for B	271
appear ＋ C	4
appoint ＋ O ＋ C	7
approach	237
arrive at ～	242
arrive in ～	242
as (関係代名詞)	153
as ...	211, 268
as ... as ～	164, 170, 176
as ... as one can	48, 170
as ... as possible	48, 170
as far as ...	212
as[so] far as ... be concerned, ...	230
as for ～	249
As for myself, ...	230
as if ...	213
as if ... 現在形 ...	70
as if ... had p.p. ...	70
as if ... 過去形 ...	70
as is often the case	153
as ＋形容詞＋ a ＋名詞 (as ～)	123, 170
as long as ...	212
as regards ～	230
as soon as ...	215, 219, 225, 268
as though ...	213
as to ～	230, 249
ask for ～	233, 244
ask ～ if ...	75, 80
ask ... not to ～	76
ask ＋ O′ ＋ O	8
ask ... to ～	76, 80
ask ～ when[who, where など] ...	75
asked if ... and said that ...	77
at all cost(s)	243
at any cost	243
at first sight	234
at noon	122
at one's disposal	239
at one's service	239
at the cost of ～	243
at the expense of ～	243
at the sight of ～	234
(at) this time tomorrow	280
a と the の区別	121
attempt to ～	68
attend	237
avoid ～ing	104, 106
awake to find ...	96
award A for B	271

291

award + O' + O		8, 271

B

B as well as A		81, 84, 235
B rather than A		169, 183
倍数の表現		168
場所を表す前置詞		228
be able to ~		64, 138
be above ~ing		193
be absent from ~		253
be acquainted with ~		225
be against ~		113
be all right with ~		60, 147, 274
be apt to ~		283
be astonished		44
be astonished to ~		98
be at a loss		97
be at a loss for ~		233
be aware of ~		224, 245
be beside oneself with ~		120, 233
be capable of ~ing		138
be conscious of ~		224, 245
be convenient for ~		60, 147, 274
be convinced of ~		229, 245
be delighted		44
be determined to ~		270
be disappointed		44
be dressed in ~		16, 225
be[get] drowned		287
be drowned to death		68
be familiar to ~		234
be familiar with ~		234
be for ~		113, 243, 274
be glad that ...		209
be going to ~		58, 88
be good at ~		140
be guilty of ~		275
be happy to ~		98
be[get] hurt		254
be ignorant of ~		245
be ~ing 〈進行形〉... when		266
be[get] injured		254
be innocent of ~		275
be interested (in ~)		44
be kind enough to ~		140
be likely to ~		88, 90, 175
be married		32
be (most) unlikely to ~		98
be obliged to A for B		272
be pleased		44
be proud of ~		141
be replaced by ~		282
be responsible for ~		236
be robbed of ~		41
be said to ...		39, 88
be satisfied that ...		209
be satisfied (with ~)		44
be shocked		44
be so kind as to ~		140
be sorry that ...		209
be sure of		245
be sure to ~		194
be surprised that ...		209
be surprised to ~		44, 98
be suspicious of ~		274
be thinking of ~ing		260
be unable to ~		64, 194
be used to ~ing		50
be worth ~ing		45, 105
be[get] wounded		254
because ...		211
Because ..., it does not follow that ...		200
because of ~		248
before ...		218
before one knows it		257
before と ago		135-136
behind one's back		272
belong to ~		273, 286
beside oneself with ~		120, 233
besides ~		235, 248
between A and B		244, 266
beyond ~		194, 200
blame A for B		247
both		125
both of which ...		158
bread and butter		83
bring － brought － brought		17, 257
bring + O' + O		3
部分否定		172, 192, 198-199, 201, 204
文型		2-10, 12-21, 36-45
分詞		102-114
分詞構文		102, 108, 109, 114, 161
文全体を修飾する副詞		141
burst into laughter		10, 123
burst into tears		10, 123
... but ...		208
buy B for A		226
buy + O' + O		3
by car[bus, train]		122, 244
by far		122, 135
by means of ~		224, 229, 248
by no means		197
by oneself		120, 233, 284
by telephone		243
by the gallon		226
by the hour		122, 226
by the month		122, 226
by the pound		122, 226
by と till, until		228
by way of ~		248

C

call ... by name		117
call for ~		233, 244
call + O + C		7, 38
can		43, 55
can do nothing but ~		256
can never ~		196
can never ~ enough		196
Can you ...?		60, 80
cannot ~ at all		196
cannot but ~		94
cannot ~ enough		205
cannot ~ for the life of me		196
cannot have p.p.		51, 55
cannot help but ~		94
cannot help ~ing		94
cannot help it		129
cannot ... too ~		196, 205
cannot ... without ~ing		110, 199, 278
care for ~		234
careful と carefully		141
catch ... by the arm		213
catch ... by the hand		13
cause ... to ~		187

cease to ～	106	
certainly	52	
charge A with B	247	
直説法と仮定法	65	
直接話法	74-80	
come from ～	3	
concerning ～	230	
consider ～ing	260	
consider + O + C	7	
convince A of B	229, 270	
convince ... to ～	270	
could have p.p.	72	
Could you ...?	60, 80, 280	
Could you kindly ...?	280	
criticize A for B	247	
CとU	142	

D

第5文型	2-10, 134
代名詞	125-131
第2文型	2-8, 134
departure for ～	246
departure from ～	246
depend on ～	224
despite ～	235
die of［from］～	228
discuss	12, 14, 237
distinguish A from B	224
distinguish between A and B	224
do（動詞）	216
do（助動詞）	50, 54
do［cause］damage (to ～)	263
do nothing but ～	93
do + S + V（原形）	50
Do you mind if ...?	106, 254
Do you mind ～ing ...?	106
do you think の位置	174, 285
don't fail to ～	194
don't have to ～	54-55
double the ～	124
動名詞	104-107, 109-111
動名詞の意味上の主語	110, 113
動名詞を目的語とする動詞	104-106
動詞	2-10, 12-21
動詞句	38-39
動詞の活用	12-18

dream of ～ing	261
dress	16
drown to death	68
during ～	227

E

each ～	85
each of which ...	158
easy to ～	283
economics	81
英文の特徴	289
英語のアクセント	9
英語の時制／日本語の時制	24
英語の主語／日本語の主語	19-21
either	125
either A or B	82
enable ... to ～	19-20
enjoy ～ing	104, 106
enough ... for ～	152
enough to ～	94, 280
enter	237
every ～	85, 118
every time ...	216
every two ～s	118
evidence	116
excuse A for B	271
exhausting と exhausted	265

F

fail in ～ing	4, 105, 194
fail to ～	194
fall－fell－fallen	50
far from ～	192-193
far into the night	245
(far) too ... to ～	287
fatal と fatally	254
feed－fed－fed	18
feel + C	4, 137, 271
feel like ～ing	110
feel + O + 原形不定詞	94
few－fewer－fewest	142
few と a few	135-136, 193, 203
find + O + C	8, 265
find + O′ + O	8
finish ～ing	104-106
flee－fled－fled	17
fling + O + C	10

flow－flowed－flowed	17
fly－flew－flown	17
for ～	113, 227, 232, 243, 274
..., for ...	211
for a good while	95
for all ～	229, 251
for breakfast	226
for fear ... should / may ～	53, 213, 220
for nothing	233, 239
for oneself	120, 233
for the purpose of ～	105, 249, 274
for ... to ～	89-90
fortunately	141
fortune と misfortune	141
free from ～	193
free of charge	233, 239
from behind ～	224
from that time on	75
from then on	75
副詞	134-138, 140-146
副詞 + V + S	84
副詞節	208, 210-220, 289
複数形にしない名詞	116, 118, 273
複数名詞の所有格	118, 130, 267
不定詞	88-99

G

原形不定詞	88, 93
現在分詞	102-114
現在完了	24, 26, 29, 31-32, 43
現在完了 ... since ～	263
get married	32
疑問文の語順	285
疑問詞	145-147
give－gave－given	18
give it up	59
give + O′ + O	3, 7
give place to	282
give up ～ing	104, 106
go for a walk	272
go on a trip［journey］	272
go on an errand	272
go on ～ing	34
go swimming［shopping］	272
誤文選択問題	271-275

誤文訂正問題	265-270	
語順に注意	170, 285	
語数指定英訳問題	285	
grab ... by the sleeve	230	
grasp ... by the hand	121	
grow up to be ...	96	
群前置詞	224, 229-230, 248	

H

had better ～	51, 58
had better have p.p.	52
had better not ～	58, 252
had p.p〈過去完了〉... when	267
half / twice as ... as ～	168
［鼻が］低い	68
［鼻が］高い	68
hang－hanged－hanged	12
hang－hung－hung	12
反語	195
happen to ～	88-90
hard to ～	177
hard と hardly	135
hardly	135, 204
hardly any ～	203
hardly ... not ～	200
hardly ... when［before］～	27, 215
have a hard time ～ing	288
have difficulty (in) ～ing	288
have good reason to ～	48-49
have got to ～	281
have no choice but to ～	256
have + O +原形不定詞	103, 113, 269
have + O + p.p.	40-42, 103, 113, 256, 264, 269
have ～ on	225
～ have passed since ...	211
have p.p. ... since ...	227, 286
have the kindness to ～	140
have to ～	38, 43, 54, 88, 281
have ～ to oneself	120
have trouble (in) ～ing	288
having p.p. ...	108

hear + O +原形 / ～ing	109
hear + O +原形不定詞	10, 37, 98, 279
hear + O + p.p.	109
hear of / hear about	13
help A with B	245
Help yourself, please.	129
Here is［are］...	128
Here you are.	128
hide－hid－hidden	30
比較	164-177
比較級 than ～	164-165, 176, 253
比較級 than any other +単数名詞	165
比較級 ... than usual	175
比較級を使わない比較	166
否定	180-205, 219
否定+比較	180-190
否定語+ as［so］... as ～	180, 190
否定語+比較級 than ～	181, 187, 189
否定語の位置	104, 108, 279
否定語を含まない否定表現	192-196
否定語を強める語句	196-197, 275
houses to live in	94
How ...?	195
How about ～ ?	147
How about ～ing?	59
How deep do you think + S + is?	285
How far is it from A to B?	145
How long ...?	145-146
How many ～s ...?	264
How many times ...?	145-146
How much ...?	146
How often ...?	145-146
How soon ...?	146
how to ～	97
how と what	145
however ... may ～	56, 214, 216

I

I am sorry ...	65
I want you to ～ .	280

I wish ...	65, 79
I'd like to ～	286
I'd like ... to ～	112-113, 280
I'd like to, but ...	93
I'd like you to ～ .	280
I'd love to, but ...	93
I'll be very happy to.	93
I'm glad to.	93
if I were you	67
if it hadn't been for ～	66, 70
if (it is) necessary	210
if it weren't for ～	66, 70
if ... ［名詞節］	75
If only ...	65-66
If ... should ～	69
If ... were to ～	69
if you like to	93
if you want to	93
imaginary	138
imaginative	138
意味上の主語	113
in addition to ～	235, 248
in case	53
in charge of ～	236
in comparison with ～	249
in favor of ～	243, 274
in ～ing	104
in no sense	197
in no way	195, 197
in one's face	272
in one's teens［twenties］	244
in opposition to ～	243
in order to ～	95
in respect of ～	230
in spite of ～	224, 235
in the afternoon	122
in vain	232, 254
inferior to ～	166, 238
information	116
instead of ～	59, 235
in と for	227
It cannot be helped.	129
it(S) ... for ... to ～	91, 99
it happened that ...	89, 90
it has been ～ since ...	26, 211
it is a pity that ... (should) ～	65-66, 131

項目	ページ
it is advisable for ... to ~	252
It is impossible for ... to ~	279
it is likely that ...	90
It is no use ~ing ...	195
it is not A but B that	221
it is not A that ... but B.	221
It is not until ~ that ...	279
it is ... of you to ~	89
it is possible for ... to ~	138
It is said that	39
it is ~ since ...	26, 211
it is ... that ...（強調構文）	84, 221
It is time	89
it(O) ... to ~	4, 93
it(S) ... to ~	91
it would be better for ... to ~	51, 252
it's a good idea to ~	51
It's (high) time ... 過去形 ...	71
It's (high) time for ... to ~ .	71

J

項目	ページ
自動詞	2-10, 12-21, 242, 287
時制	24-34, 74-80
助動詞	48-61
助動詞＋have p.p.	51-53
受動態	36-45
受動態の時制による形	37
受動態と文型	36-45
jump to one's feet	117
junior to ~	166, 238
従位接続詞	208
従属節	208

K

項目	ページ
書き出し指定完成問題	256-258
過去分詞	102-114
過去分詞 ..., S ＋ V ＋ X ＋ X.	109
過去完了	24, 27-28, 30-32
過去完了 ... since ~	263
格変化	116, 119, 150
関係代名詞	257
関係代名詞と関係副詞	161

項目	ページ
関係詞	150-162, 289
関係副詞	150, 153-154
完了形	24-34
完了形の分詞構文	108
間接話法	74-80
冠詞の有無	116, 121-124
仮定法	64-72, 77, 213
仮定法過去	64-72, 187-188
仮定法過去完了	64-72
数の概念	116-130
数の一致	81-85, 262-263
keep ＋ C	5
keep ... from ~ing	19
keep ~ to oneself	120
形容詞	134-144, 148
形容詞 ..., S ＋ V ＋ X ＋ X.	109
結果を表す不定詞	96, 254
祈願文	77
金額	83
kiss ... on the lips	13, 230
know A from B	224
know better	193
know better than to ~	193
後置修飾	289
口語と文語	253
高低アクセント	99
固有名詞と定冠詞	267
句と節	253
強弱アクセント	99

L

項目	ページ
large と many	138
late into the night	245
late－later－latest	135
late－latter－last	135
late と latter	135
lay－laid－laid // laying	15, 17
lean against ~	227, 272
leave	237
leave ... in one's care[in the care of ~]	249
lest ... should ~	52-53, 213, 220
Let's ..., shall we?	60
lie－lay－lain // lying	15, 17, 29
like ~ing	109
like to ~	109

項目	ページ
listen to ~	39, 44
little－less－least	142
live to be ...	96
long と short	138
look after ~	141, 234
look at ~	13, 224
look ＋ C	4, 6, 137
look for ~	233, 244
look forward to ~ing	105
look ... in the face	13, 213, 230
look into ~	13, 224
look on ~	224
look over ~	224
lots of ~	143
luckily	141

M

項目	ページ
紛らわしい名詞	117
major in ~	265
make an attempt to ~	68
make effort	71
make little of ~	44, 284
make much of ~	44, 284
make much use of ~	39
make nothing of ~	284
make ＋ O ＋原形不定詞	20, 37
make ＋ O ＋ p.p.	283
make oneself understood	103, 283, 288
make up ~	229
make up for ~	229
many a ~	84
many ~s	84
many－more－most	142
many と much	135-136, 142-143
marry	12, 14, 237
まさか	148
mathematics	81
may	52
may have p.p.	51
May I ...?	55, 61, 147
may not ~	55
may well ~	48-49, 55-56
maybe	52
命令文 ... and ...	208
命令文 ... or ...	208

295

mention	12, 14, 237	
might as well ~	51, 253	
might well ~	49, 55-56	
mind ~ing	104, 106, 254	
未来完了	24-25, 29	
未来形	25	
未来に対する条件・仮定	69	
目的格＋~ing	113	
more and more of which ...	159	
more than ... can ~	194	
most ~s	123	
most of the ~s	123	
......, much[still] more ~	165	
much – more – most	142	
無冠詞	260	
must	43, 281	
must have p.p.	51-52, 56-57	
mustn't / must not ~	55	
my ~ing	106	

N

name ＋ O ＋ C	8
narrow と small	137
naturally	141
near ~	238
near to ~	238
nearer to ~	238
nearest to ~	238
need ~ing	45, 105
need not ~	55
need not have p.p.	51-52
neither	125-126, 198
neither A nor B	82
Neither V ＋ S.	209
never ... as ... as ~	176
never fail to ~	194
never ... 比較級 than ~	176, 185
never ... so ... as ~	176
never ... such a ... as ~	176
never to ~	96
never ... without ~ing	199, 278
日本語と英語	2, 9, 19, 287, 289
二重否定	192, 199-204, 278
no ... except ~	201
no 比較級 ... than ~	189
no less than	182

no less ... than ~	185
no matter how ... may ~	56, 214, 216-217
no matter what ... may ~	56
no matter where ... may ~	217
no matter who may ~	216
no more than ~	182, 187-188, 190
no more ... than ~	181, 185, 188
no other ... is 比較級 than ~	165
No sooner ... than ~.	215
no ... whatever	275
none	125-126
..., nor V ＋ S.	209
not A but B	221, 235
not ... all ~	198, 204, 261
not always ~	199, 204
not ... any ~	198
not ... any more than ~	181, 185, 188
not as ... as ~	190
not ... at all	192, 197, 203, 275
not ... both	198
not ... either	136, 198
not ..., either	201, 203
not ... every ~	198, 204
not ... everything	201
not exactly	199
not 比較級 than ~	182, 190
not ... hopeless	201
not ... in any way	195
not ... in the least	197, 275
not less than ~	182
not less ... than ~	185
not ......, let alone ~	166
not more than ~	182
not more ... than ~	185
not ......, much[still] less ~	165
not necessarily	199
not ..., nor V ＋ S	203
not only A but B	81, 84, 235
not really ~	271
not ... simply because ~	219
not so ... as ~	190, 253
not so much A as B	169, 183
not so much as ...	183

not ... till ~	32
not to ~	279
not ... until ~	10, 279
not until ... V ＋ S	10
not ... whatever	197
nothing but ~	226
Nothing ... 比較級 than ~.	187
nothing less than ~	186
nothing more than ~	186
能動態	36-45

O

object to ~ing	111
of itself	120
of one's own ~ing	111, 252
おいしい	148
おもしろい	148
on account of ~	248
on delivery	225
on errands	272
on ~ing	104, 110, 225, 235
on one's foot	117
on one's knees	117
on one's left	238
on the ceiling	246
on the telephone	243
on the wall	246
on top of ~	248
one / ones	125-127
one of the ~s	119
one's absence from ~	253
one's company	273-274
one's fears for ~	240
oneself	119
only to ~	96, 232, 254
others	125, 127
ought not to ~	58
ought to ~	50-51, 58, 252
ought to have p.p.	51
over the telephone	243
owing to ~	248

P

pat ... on the shoulder	121, 230
pay A for B	226
perhaps	52
physics	81

plenty of ～	95, 144	
point out	41	
politics	81	
praise A for B	247	
prayed that ... might ～	77	
prefer A to B	166	
press ... against ～	272	
prevent ... from ～ing	19	
pride oneself on ～	141	
pride と proud	140	
probably	52	
propose to ... that ... should ～		77
punch ... on the nose	213, 230	
punish A for B	247	
put it off	59	
put on	16	
put up with	38	

R

raise‐raised‐raised	16
rarely	204
reach	237
real と really	266
regardless of A, B or C	262
remain ＋ C	5
remember ～ing	109
remember to ～	109
remind A of B	12, 15, 21, 278
連立完成問題	251
reply to	13
reproach A for B	247
resemble	237
respectable	138
respectful	138
respective	138
result from ～	274
result in ～	274
rise‐rose‐risen	16, 30
rob	13, 18
rob A of B	13-14, 18, 42
room for ～	95

S

S ＋ be p.p.	6
S ＋ be p.p. ＋ C	6
S ＋ be p.p. ＋ O	6
S′＋(being/having been)＋p.p.	108
S ＋ V ＋ C	2-8, 36, 137
S ＋ V (＋ M)	2, 3, 6, 36
S ＋ V ＋ O	2, 5-6, 8, 10, 36
S ＋ V ＋ O ＋ C	2-10, 36, 40, 137, 156
S ＋ V ＋ O ＋～ing	103
S ＋ V ＋ O′＋ O	2, 3, 6-8, 36, 40
S ＋ V ＋ O ＋ p.p.	103
said (that) ... and that ...	76
said (that) ... but that ...	76
最上級の文脈による意味	172
save A from B	244
scarcely	136, 204
Scarcely ... when［before］～.	215
scold A for B	247
search と search for	151, 233, 244
seat‐seated‐seated	16
see ＋ O ＋原形不定詞	37, 260, 269
see ＋ O ＋～ing	44, 102, 269
see ＋ O ＋ p.p.	102
seem ＋ C	4
seem to ...	88
正誤判定問題	260-264
整序問題	278-284
seldom / rarely	136, 204
sell well	45
send for ～	233
send ＋ O′＋ O	7
senior to ～	166, 238
先行詞	156-158, 257
先行詞＋［形容詞句/副詞句］＋関係詞 ...	157-158
選択完成問題	242
set ... free	3
set ＋ O ＋ C	3
接続詞	208-221, 227
Shall I ...?	147
Shall we ...?	60
進行形	24-25, 28-29, 34
進行形の受動態	36-37
進行形にしない動詞	273
…してから～になる	26, 32
should	39, 131, 252
should have p.p.	51, 65
show ＋ O ＋ O	3
所有格 ＋ ～ing	106, 113
主節	208
since ～(～以来)	26, 211
since ...(…であるから)	211
sit‐sat‐sat	16
smell ＋ C	7
...., so ...	208, 215
so ... as ～	164, 170, 176
so as to ～	95
so far as ...	212
so ＋形容詞＋ a ～	123, 170
so long as ...	212
so ... may not ～	213
so ... that ...	55, 64 214
..., so that ...	215
so that ... can ～	55, 90
so ... that ... cannot ～	91, 192
so that ... may ～	55
so that ... may not ～	213, 220
.... So ＋ V ＋ S.	203
some ... others ～	127
soon after ...	219, 268
sound ＋ C	8
speak of［about］～	238
stay ＋ C	5
steal	13, 18, 42
steal‐stole‐stolen	13, 18
stop ... from ～ing	19
stop ～ing	104, 106
stop to ～	106
strike ... on the head	13, 121, 213
strong と weak	138
すばらしい	148
substitute B for A	282
succeed in ～ing	4, 105
such a ～	123
such ... as ～	153, 257
such ... that ...	214
suggest to ... that ... should ～	77
suit	60, 147
superior to ～	166, 238
surely	52

T

他動詞	2-10, 12-21, 237, 287
take	20
take ... by the arm	230

take care of ～	41, 238	
take charge of ～	38	
take it easy	67	
take off	16	
take pride in ～	141	
take the place of	282	
take－took－taken	17	
talk of［about］～	14, 238	
単数・複数	81-85, 116-130, 262	
taste＋C	7	
teach＋O′＋O	7	
tell A from B	224	
tell ... not to ～	76	
tell ... to ～	76	
thank A for B	271	
thanks to ～	248	
than を使わない比較表現	238	
that ... may not ～	213	
that of ～	126	
that ... should ～	212	
the exchange rate of A to B	242	
the 比較級 of the two	164	
the 比較級 ..., the 比較級 ...	143, 169, 171-172, 175, 269-270	
(the) Japanese (people)	263	
the＋形容詞	82	
the last ... that ...	196	
the last ... to ～	98, 196	
the love of A for B	240	
the moment ...	215, 219, 268	
the more ..., the more ～	143, 175	
the Netherlands	81	
the night before	74	
the number of ～	83	
the other	125, 127	
the Philippines	81	
the previous night	74	
the 最上級	166, 172	
the 最上級 of all	164	
the 最上級 of all the ～s	165	
the 最上級 ～ that ... ever ...	176	
the second 最上級	166	
the United States	81	
there is ... ～ing	112	
There is no ～ing.	110	
there is nothing for it but to ～	256	
there is ... p.p.	112	
There V＋S.	82	
there's no use (in) ～ing	195, 201	
They say (that)	39	
thick と thin	138	
think highly of ～	284	
think little of ～	284	
think much of ～	284	
think nothing of ～	284	
think＋O＋C	9	
those	85, 125-126, 158	
those of ～	126	
those ～ which ...	158	
those ～ who ...	85, 158	
through ～	225	
till ...	220, 256	
～ times as ... as ～	168, 174	
to be frank (with you)	88	
to change the subject	88	
to have p.p.（完了形不定詞）	90	
to no avail	232	
to one's face	272	
to one's left	238	
to oneself	233	
to tell (you) the truth	88	
toast and butter	83	
時を表す副詞節	25-26, 29, 268	
時を表す前置詞	228	
too	136	
too＋形容詞＋a＋名詞 (to ～)	124	
too ... to ～	91, 192, 200	
等位［対等］接続詞	208	
try ～ing	109	
try to ～	68, 109	
twice a week	121	
twice as long as ～	124	
twice the ～	124	

U

under consideration	246	
under construction	246	
unfortunately	141	
unless ...	30, 212	
unluckily	141	
until ...	220, 256	
used to ～	49, 114, 251	

V

very と much	135	
via ～	248	

W

話法	74-80	
wait for ... to ～	94	
want ～ing	45, 105	
want＋O＋to ～	112-113	
want ... to ～	279-280	
watch＋O＋原形不定詞	10	
wear－wore－worn	16	
well と good	140	
what（関係代名詞）	150, 152, 154	
What has become of ～?	29, 232	
What has he become?	29	
What is the use of ～ing ...?	195	
what it is like to ～	127	
What time ...?	147	
what to ～	97, 210	
whatever ... may ～	56, 217	
when（関係副詞）	153, 161	
when ...	210, 261	
When ...?	147	
when it is convenient (for you)	261	
when to ～	97, 210	
whenever ...	110, 216	
where（関係副詞）	153-154, 160, 257	
Where is this?	128	
where to ～	97	
wherever ... may ～	217	
whether ...	75	
whether ... or not	281	
whether to ～ or not	97, 210	
... which ～	257	
..., which ...	150, 152, 157	
which book to read	97	
Which day ...?	147	
which way to ～	65, 97	
while ...	210, 218, 227, 256	
Who ...?	195	
..., who ...	150, 152	

who – whose – whom		150-151
whoever ...		150, 154
whoever may ~		216
whom to ~		97
whose roof ... / the roof of which ...		151, 252
why（関係副詞）		162
Why don't you ...?		54
wide と large		137
will be ~ing		280
will have to ~		256
will not ~		56
wind – wound – wound		30
with a score of A to B		242
with a view to ~ing		105, 249, 274
with admiration		76
with all ~		229, 251
with delight		76
with reference to ~		230
with respect to ~		230
with surprise		76
with the view of ~ing		274
without ~		66, 70
without avail		232
without knowing it		257
without so much as ...		183
without success		232, 254
「…を～される」		41-42
won't ~		56
would not ~		56
would often ~		49, 114, 251
Would you ...?		60, 106, 254, 280
Would you be kind enough to ~?		280
Would you kindly ...?		280
Would you mind if ...?		254
Would you mind if ... 過去形 ...?		106
Would you mind ~ing ...?		106
wound – wounded – wounded		30
write (to) ~		286

Z

全部否定	198
前置詞	224-240
前置詞＋関係代名詞	150-151, 154, 160-162
前置詞が不要な他動詞	237
前置詞句	224
前置詞＋名詞	224, 289
前置詞の有無など	237-238

山口 俊治　Shunji YAMAGUCHI

日本医科大学元教授　東京大学英文科卒業

「受験生から受ける質問で答えられないものは一切ない」という英語への確固たる自信を20代で早くも築く。

今日の英語指導の根幹を形成する"ネクサス"の解明を始めとする『山口英文法講義の実況中継』の斬新な講義内容は，受験参考書の枠を超え，読者の知的財産として，生涯役立つことは確かだ。その幅広い学識から溢れるユーモアを交えた講義の名調子は英語そのものの理解を一段と深めてくれるに相違ない。

＊　　　＊　　　＊

著作：『NEW 山口英文法講義の実況中継』，『総合英文読解ゼミ』，『英単語 Make it!(全2冊)』，『英会話 Make it!(全2冊)』，『英熟語イディオマスター』，『あたりまえながらなぜ英単語はすぐ忘れてしまうのか？』(以上，語学春秋社)，『英語構文全解説』(研究社)など多数。

趣味：囲碁(七段格)，ドライブ，写真など

教科書をよむ前によむ! 3日で読める!
実況中継シリーズ がパワーアップ!!

シリーズ売上累計1,000万部を超えるベストセラー参考書『実況中継』が，読みやすい装丁になって続々登場! ますますわかりやすくなって，使いやすさも抜群です。

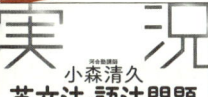

英語

小森清久
英文法・語法問題講義の実況中継
定価(本体1,300円+税)

文法・語法・熟語・イディオム・発音・アクセント・会話表現の入試必出7ジャンル対策を1冊にまとめた決定版。ポイントを押さえた詳しい解説と1050問の最新の頻出問題で，理解力と解答力が同時に身につきます。

西きょうじ
図解英文読解講義の実況中継
定価(本体1,200円+税)

高校1，2年生レベルの文章から始めて，最後には入試レベルの論説文を読み解くところまで読解力を引き上げます。英文を読むための基本事項を1つひとつマスターしながら進むので，無理なく実力がUPします。

大矢復
英作文講義の実況中継
定価(本体1,200円+税)

日本語的発想のまま英文を書くと，正しい英文とズレが生じて入試では命取り。その原因 ―誰もが誤解しがちな"文法""単語"― を明らかにして，入試英作文を完全攻略します。自由英作文対策も万全。

大矢復
図解英語構文講義の実況中継

定価（本体 1,200 円+税）

高校生になったとたんに英文が読めなくなった人におすすめ。英文の仕組みをヴィジュアルに解説するので，文構造がスッキリわかって，一番大事な部分がハッキリつかめるようになります。

石井雅勇
センターリスニング講義の実況中継

CD2枚付　定価（本体 1,600 円+税）

センター試験を分析し，その特徴と対策を凝縮した1冊。予想問題で本番と同じ雰囲気も味わえます。日本人とネイティヴの音の違いをまとめた「速効耳トレ!」パートも分かりやすいと評判です。

国語

山村由美子
図解古文読解講義の実況中継

定価（本体 1,200 円+税）

古文のプロが時間と労力をかけてあみだした正しく読解をするための公式 "ワザ85" を大公開。「なんとなく読んでいた」→「自信を持って読めた」→「高得点GET」の流れが本書で確立します。

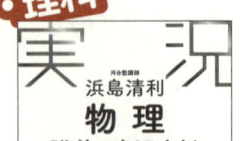

理科

浜島清利
物理講義の実況中継 [物理基礎＋物理]

定価（本体 2,100 円+税）

力学・熱・波動・電磁気・原子の5ジャンルをまとめて収録。物理で大切な「考え方」を身につけ，精選された良問で応用力まで飛躍します。1問ごとにパワーアップを実感する1冊です。

実況中継シリーズは順次刊行予定！詳しくはホームページで！
http://goshun.com　語学春秋　検索　2014年5月現在